Plans of 1918 remodel of the Lane County courthouse.
From the Lane County Historical Society collection

Rebellion, Murder and a Pulitzer Prize

The 1933 Murder Trial of Llewellyn Banks, Leader of the Jackson County Rebellion

By Joe R. Blakely

Author of

Lifting Oregon Out Of The Mud;
Building the Oregon Coast Highway 1936-1966; and
OSWALD WEST - Governor of Oregon 1911-1915

First Edition, 2015

Cover photo:
Jackson County Courthouse - c1940.
Photo from Southern Oregon Historical Society

Back Cover photo:
Lane County Courthouse, 1905
Photo from Lane County Historical Society

Published by
Groundwaters Publishing, LLC

P.O. Box 50, Lorane, Oregon 97451
http://www.groundwaterspublishing.com

ISBN-13: 978-1517707460
ISBN-10: 1517707463

Preface

One night while reading *Oregon's Main Street: U.S. Highway 99*, written by Jo-Brew and Pat Edwards, I discovered a story they had excerpted from Ben Truwe's website, "Capsule Histories," concerning the Jackson County Rebellion, in 1933. As I investigated, I found out that at the climax of the Rebellion, a police officer was murdered while trying to arrest a wealthy newspaper publisher.

It sounded like an interesting story. The trial was moved from Jackson County to Lane County's courthouse in Eugene. I told myself that if I could find a transcript of that trial, I would prepare a book.Much to my surprise, I found it – possibly the last copy – at the Oregon State Archives. In the file with the transcript was a bloody arrest warrant, still covered with Officer Prescott's blood. I photographed it, and put it back into the file.

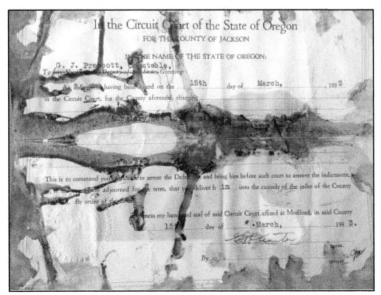

Bloody arrest warrant - *From the Oregon State Archives*

As a result, my book includes actual trial excerpts from 1933. As the murder trial unfolds I tell the story of the Jackson County Rebellion.

Robert Ruhl, editor of the *Medford Mail Tribune,* wrote in his paper on October 29, 1921:

"So we come to the somewhat righteous conclusion—that the difference between happiness and misery in this life is largely the difference between building up character and allowing character to go to seed. It is an old lesson as old as the world, but is a tremendously valuable one to remember and a tremendously costly one too forget."

Table of Contents

Introduction

A Jackson County, Oregon grand jury indicted Llewellyn Banks and Edith Banks for murder in the first degree on March 24, 1933, charging that Mr. Banks shot Constable George Prescott at Banks' home in Medford, Oregon on March 16th. The trial would normally have taken place in Medford, but Banks' attorneys complained that there was unreasonable prejudice against their client in Jackson County. Medford was the home of the well-liked constable. Furthermore the defense attorney claimed the press, especially the *Medford Mail Tribune* and the *Jacksonville Miner*, had published defamatory, scandalous, and highly prejudicial statements. Circuit Court Judge G.F. Skipworth approved the change and the case was moved to the Lane County Circuit Courthouse in Eugene, Oregon, where the murder trial commenced on May 1, 1933.

The following is an excerpt from that trial's transcript. Under direct-examination by defense attorney Frank Lonergan, Mr. Banks described what had happened when Constable George Prescott tried to arrest him on that fateful morning of March 16, 1933.

The Shooting

Q. And then what happened?

A. Then when the knock came on the door, I could not see from where I sat who was at the door, so I got up and looked through the door.

Q. How do you mean you looked through the door?

A. Well, the window in the door was about five feet---

Q. Well, you looked through the window then?

A. I looked through the window and I had to walk up to the door to look through it because you couldn't see through it any distance away, and I saw that it was George Prescott, and a plainclothes man. These plainclothes men had been making most of the arrests.

Q. Did you know the man that was with Mr. Prescott at the time?

A. No, I didn't recognize him.

Q. Did you know Sergeant O'Brien around Medford?

A. I knew of him.

Q. You didn't know him personally?

A. I had written articles about him, but I had never met him, but as I saw Mr. Prescott, my mind went to Walker. I didn't know that it was Walker.

Q. That is, you mean when you saw Prescott you thought Prescott was Walker?

A. No, I know Mr. Prescott very well, but the plainclothes man, my mind just went to Walker.

Q. Who was Walker, the state police?

A. Walker, I have never met him. I didn't know him, but was told that Walker was going to shoot L. A. Banks on sight.

Q. You thought that was the one that was with Prescott?

A. I just expected it, yes.

Q. What did you do then?

A. I said to Mr. Fleming, I said, "The officers are here and you had better leave." I didn't wait to see what Fleming did. Things were very tense at that moment. I left for the kitchen. I walked out into the kitchen. Mrs. Banks was washing dishes, the breakfast dishes, she had her apron on and her hands were in the dishwater. I asked her if she would take those two letters and pass them through the door to these officers, but I said, "Put the door on the chain and under no circumstances permit these officers to enter the house." Mrs. Banks moved very rapidly, generally, I mean naturally. She took off her apron and dried her hands and started for the front entrance of the living room. As she – I walked with her to the door. (Witness is down before State's Exhibit I, the plat on the blackboard) Mrs. Banks was at the sink here, right here. I believe there is a table in the kitchen right here, right there. (Indicating on State's Exhibit I)

Q. Indicating the westerly end of the kitchen?

A. Yes, there was a table right there, Mrs. Banks dried her hands and put her apron on that table. She continued on through—

Q. Indicating a door?

A. That door leads from the pantry into the hallway. Mrs. Banks went on through to the table and got the letters, I suppose. I didn't see that but I know she did. I turned in here, went back to the day bed, and picked up my rifle.

Q. Then what did you do?

A. I walked to the front entrance of the house. When I first arrived in the room Mrs. Banks had her hands through the door. I believe that she was passing out those letters.

Q. You say you walked to the front part of the house? What do you mean?

A. (Witness down before the plat) I walked from here to this gate, swinging gate.

Q. Swinging gate?

A. Swinging door, swings both ways. This hallway is not built all the way up. You see it is only that high. (Indicating) And I walked through here to a point I should say about there. (Indicating)

Q. Indicating about where you were sitting when you talked with Mr. Fleming?

A. Very near to where I was sitting. Perhaps I was back a little further, perhaps that far back.

Q. All right.

A. (Witness resuming stand) And as I saw Mrs. Banks passing these letters as I supposed through that door, I saw Mr. Prescott or I saw a foot, who I believe was Mr. Prescott's foot, in the jamb of the door. Then Mrs. Banks was pressing on that door with all her force. (Witness standing up) And she said, "You shall not come in, you shall not come in." That's what she was saying when I came in the room or immediately thereafter. Then the door on a chain, I am at an angle to the chain, the opening, at an angle can scarcely be seen. But that opening was widening perceptibly, as Mrs. Banks was pushing on the door.

Q. Well now, you say when you came out from the hallway there into the dining room, out into the living room there and indicated approximately the place were you were, you saw Mrs. Banks reaching through the door? Then you saw the foot of someone come in. Did you see anything else beside the foot at that time?

A. I was just going to tell you that. The door was gradually widening, the opening, and I saw what I believed to be a pistol. I couldn't see who held it because I couldn't see any person excepting the very small crack in that door. (Witness is down before plat) It is very important it seems to me. Now, this door opens up this way, and standing here--

Q. When you say it opens up this way, now, you mean that the door swings in and to the left as you face the house?

A. Yes, sir. If you were on this side of that door, you couldn't see through the door, or if you are directly in front of it you couldn't see through the door with the door open at four inches, off at that angle, by reason of this corner—

Q. Indicating the corner of the vestibule?

A. Northeast corner, by reason of the corner of the vestibule, it is very difficult to see through there under any circumstances but the door was commencing to widen. (Witness resumes witness stand) I believed at that instant that the door would break open any instant. That's what I thought. In fact, there was all the evidence in the world in my mind that in just another instant the door would burst open. Mrs. Banks was struggling with all her might against the door and calling to them, "You shall not come in." I called out in a voice I believe they could hear four blocks. That may be too strong. But I called in a very loud voice, "Get away from that door." Twice. But the door was still coming in. I raised my rifle and shot as near as possible through the door..."

5

Battle for Power

The May 1, 1933 trial in Eugene, Oregon was not simply a trial for murder. The shooting had been part of a larger plot—a dramatic struggle to gain control of Jackson County government. Leaders of the right wing Good Government Congress wanted an all-out revolution, a rebellion that would replace elected officials with a dictator. The Great Depression had brought desperate times to the country. Elsewhere in the world, governments were falling to tyrants like Hitler and Mussolini. The United States battled insurgencies too, and in some instances demagogues shouted their way to power, often flouting the laws and killing or ruining popularly elected officials. In Jackson County a small group of men sought to overturn the government by inciting poorer county inhabitants to rise up against the wealthy urban elected leadership.

This fight for power was well reported in Jackson County's newspapers. Newspapers were the most important form of news coverage in the United States at that time. In Medford the battle lines were drawn between the *Medford Daily News*, a daily morning paper owned by Llewellyn A. Banks; and the *Medford Mail Tribune*, an evening daily owned and edited by Robert Ruhl. *The Daily News* fought to remove elected officials while the *Mail Tribune* fought for established law and order.

The battle to rule Jackson County led to the killing of a popular police officer, George Prescott. The *Medford Mail Tribune* won a Pulitzer Prize for its coverage of this sensational story.

Some claimed that the Jackson County rebellion led Sinclair Lewis to write his famous novel, *It Can't Happen Here*.

Leadership

G.F. Skipworth.
Photo from the Lane County Historical Society collection

Judge G.F. Skipworth presided over the Eugene Trial. Skipworth was midway through his successful career as judge of Oregon's second district, which covered southwestern Oregon. He was no novice in leading lawyers, witnesses and the public through high-profile murder trials. He had tried the first case in the Lane County Courthouse after the building had been remodeled in 1918. During his long tenure in Lane County he had championed a local juvenile court. When the county's first juvenile detention home was opened in 1950, it was named after Judge Skipworth.

Times were hard in Oregon in 1933. The Depression had led to unemployment and great suffering. But at least for a while Oregonians could take their minds off of their own hardships by focusing on the lurid murder trial of Llewellyn Banks, a wealthy orchardist and newspaper publisher.

Banks was no newcomer to politics. In 1929 under the Independent banner, he had challenged incumbent Charles McNary for one of Oregon's seats in the U.S. senate. Banks had railed against the federal farm board, banking interests, and Wall Street. Though he lost his run for senator it may have whetted his appetite for political power.

Llewellyn Banks' love of money had also become a subject of public discussion. He had two Cadillac's in his garage. When in town he wore finely tailored suits and draped Mrs. Banks in mink wraps. Meanwhile, an actual bank was said to be foreclosing on his home because of unpaid liens.

Given this level of notoriety, Llewellyn Banks and his wife Edith were chaperoned by police guards, into Eugene with the level of publicity usually reserved for celebrated movie stars. Their dressing rooms, however, lacked Hollywood glamour. Llewellyn was housed in the county jail. Edith stayed in the city jail. There they remained, just a few days, until the trial opened.

The Lane County Courthouse

The Lane County Courthouse, c1930.
Photo from the Lane County Historical Society collection

Inside clock tower with clock mechanism. *Photo from the Lane County Historical Society collection*

L ane County's 35-year-old courthouse was a stately three-story building between Oak Street and E. Park fronting on E. 8th Avenue. The exterior sported brick and a stone foundation. Embedded on the front wall was a six-by-six-foot cement relief displaying the scales of justice. Spanish tiles, two skylights, and chimneys graced the roof. A clock tower topped the attic and above that—a lightening pole. The noble Osburn Hotel stood across E. Park and the county jail across Oak Street to the west. A Spanish-American war memorial occupied the southwest corner of the courthouse block. Front cement steps led up and under the arched entry to a porch. Huge wooden doors opened onto a vestibule. From there it wasn't far to the stairway that led up to the second floor. Once on the second floor people walked north down a long corridor to a set of double doors; inside these doors was the courtroom, where Banks' murder trial would be held.

Osburn Hotel, 1931
Photo from the Lane County Historical Society collection

The Lane County Jail,1926
*Photo from the Lane County
Historical Society collection*

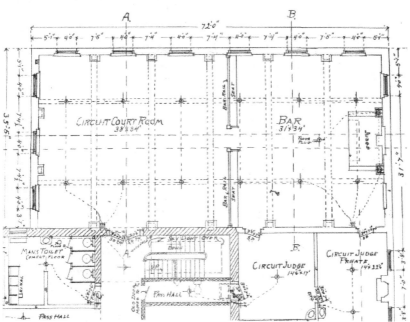

Plans of new circuit courtroom, 1918.
From the Lane County Historical Society collection

The Trial –
May 1 through May 6, 1933

May 1, 1933

The huge circuit court courtroom was sixty-nine feet by thirty-four feet. The judge presided from an elevated platform at the east end. Above and behind him was a three-foot tall statue of Lady Justice with the scales of justice in her left hand and a raised sword in the right. Along the north and west walls were sculptures of famous people on pedestals between windows trimmed with oak. Ornate oak wainscoting skirted the room. Chandeliers hung from the ceiling. The defense attorneys, along with the defendants were seated in the Bar section, east of a two-foot tall room divider. The spectators sat behind the Bar railing in the circuit court room and were not allowed in the Bar section.

Frank Lonergan, attorney for Llewellyn Banks. *Photo courtesy of the Oregon State Library, Salem*

Lady Justice inside the Lane County Courthouse; date unknown. *Photo from the Lane County Historical Society collection*

Lady Justice, 1918
*From the Lane County Historical
Society collection*

The defense lawyers for this trial were as famous as the Medford couple accused of murder. Representing Llewellyn and Edith Banks were five attorneys. Frank J. Lonergan of Portland was a long-time member of the Oregon state legislature who had served as speaker of the house in 1932. In his younger days he had been an acclaimed running back for Notre Dame. Later he had coached track and baseball in Portland, and had been a standout amateur football player with Multnomah's Athletic Club. He served as chairman of the Portland boxing association for many years. By the time of the Banks' trial, he had a reputation as one of the cleverest defense lawyers in the state. The second of the Banks' defense attorneys was William Phipps, former editor and publisher of the *Medford Clarion* (1920-1924) a newspaper that had notoriously aligned itself with the Ku Klux Klan. The remaining three defense lawyers were T.J. Enright of Medford, Joseph L. Hammersly of Portland, and Charles A. Hardy from Eugene.

Four attorneys represented the State of Oregon for the prosecution. William S. Levens was an assistant Attorney General who had been selected by Governor Meier to lead the state's case. Ralph Elmo Moody, also an assistant Attorney General had served as assistant United States Attorney General during both the Harding and Coolidge administrations. He was the son of a former Oregon governor, Z.F. Moody, and was a former member of the Oregon House of Representatives. Many considered Moody one of the most colorful attorneys in the state. Also prosecuting for the state was George A. Codding, district attorney of Jackson County; and G.W. Neilson, his deputy district attorney.

Ralph Moody, 1895
Photo from the Oregon State Library, Salem

While the attorneys sat in their high-backed oak chairs, shuffling papers at their massive rectan-

Ralph Moody, Assistant Attorney General in 1935
Photo from the Oregon Historical Society collection

gular oak tables, more than 200 spectators crowded behind them in the courtroom. Every section of society was there, from common laborers to businessmen in high-priced suits. Mingled in between were newspapermen, photographers, and future lawyers. Typical Eugene weather greeted them on opening day with overcast skies and showers. The courtroom windows were open, so the spectators could see and smell the dampness.

Sitting directly behind the defense lawyers were the stars of the show, Llewellyn and Edith Banks. According to a newspaper report, Mr. Banks was nattily dressed in a gray suit, leaning back on his chair's wooden legs, tapping his fingers on the armrest. Mrs. Banks smiled often and wore a mink wrap, seemingly unaware

Llewellyn Banks
From the Southern Oregon Historical Society collection

that if her lawyers were to lose the case she would be sentenced to death. Next to them were Llewellyn's brother-in-law and sister Mr. and Mrs. George Moran of Cleveland, Ohio.

Judge Skipworth wasted little time commanding order and starting the trial. It had been determined that both Llewellyn and his wife would be prosecuted together for the same crime, although the jury could come back with separate verdicts for each defendant.

The process for selecting jurors began immediately. As the jurors presented themselves, the defense asked questions that suggested where their case was headed. Did the juror's think a citizen might feel threatened enough to shoot a policeman in self-defense? Could the government persecute citizens? Did the jurors believe someone might be temporarily insane when pulling a trigger? During the first day most of the jury had been selected, but challenges to that selection still remained for both the defense and the state.

May 2, 1933

In the morning on the second day of the trial state lawyers and defense attorneys questioned more jurors. The state was without its lead attorney William S. Levens, who had not been feeling well. Attorney Ralph E. Moody took over the questioning. As the jurors were questioned some had amusing replies that tickled the spectators in the crowded courtroom. Judge Skipworth had to rap his gavel more then once to maintain order. The defendants Llewellyn Banks in his light gray Norfolk suit, and Edith in her seal skin coat, laughed too. No doubt their amusement didn't last long as the state's attorneys made it clear the outcome for the defendants.

That afternoon the court was stunned to learn the state's lead attorney W.S. Levens died suddenly of a heart attack in a doctor's office after his morning illness. Ralph E. Moody took over as the lead attorney for the state on Levens' death.

By 3pm the jury had been accepted and sworn in. The jury was comprised of six women—all of them housewives—and six men— including two farmers, one engineer, one laborer, one millworker, and one retired man. The two alternates were both men.

The judge addressed the jurors: "Let the record show that this jury had been duly empanelled and sworn and it is the order of the Court that the jury be kept together in charge of two bailiffs, Mr. Thomas S. Wells, and Mrs. Thomas Bailey, and that the Sheriff is hereby ordered to provide suitable quarters for the jury. I want to repeat what I have said now to the jury about the importance of this case, and the importance of the jury not to have any contacts in any wise with anybody in connection with this case, and I hope you will make it easy for the bailiffs who have charge of the jury. If you men smoke, why, the bailiffs will provide whatever tobacco you want and whatever comforts you need you make it known to the bailiffs and they will make it just as comfortable for you as is possible under the circumstances."

The jury was quartered on the fifth floor of the Osburn Hotel in

The Osburn Hotel room
Photo from the Lane County Historical Society collection

rooms conveniently located across the street from the courthouse. Their meals would be served in the hotel's dining room. The jury could take walks downtown but only in the accompaniment of the bailiffs. Outside contact was kept to a minimum. Should a jury member want word from home, the bailiff did the calling and would pass on the information to the jurist. When the lawyers for both the prosecution and the defense had completed their cases, Judge Skipworth would issue instructions to the jury. They would then be led up to the jury room on the third floor of the courthouse, where they would discuss the case and determine the verdict. The room had a large rectangular table with 12 chairs. Whenever the bailiffs wanted to enter the jury room they would have to announce themselves. If the case was not resolved by nighttime the jury would have to spend the night in the courthouse. Two adjacent rooms, separated for men and women had 12 single beds with clean blankets and linen.

May 3, 1933

(The jury has been selected. On this day begins the transcript of the trial.)

At 1:30 pm on Wednesday the court read the indictment against the Banks: "Llewellyn A. Banks and Edith Banks are accused by the grand jury of the county of Jackson, state of Oregon, by this indictment of the crime of murder in the first degree." The Banks' appeared unmoved. The jury, on the other hand, leaned forward and listened intently.

After both the prosecution and the defense agreed that witnesses should be excluded from the courtroom until after they had testified, Judge Skipworth announced, "All witnesses must retire from the courtroom. Have the courtroom quiet down." As soon as the witnesses left their seats were quickly filled by spectators who had been crowded in the hallway, and down the stairs to the courthouse lobby on the first floor. "The courtroom is full," The judge told the bailiffs, don't let anybody else in. No use to let anyone else in." Finally the doors to the courtroom were closed. The judge said to the state lawyers, "Make your opening statement."

Drawings of doors to courtroom, 1918
From the Lane County Historical Society collection

Ralph Moody began: "Banks killed Prescott. Mrs. Banks assisted him. They knew he was an officer of the law serving legal papers, and his death had been carefully mapped out in advance. They had warned Prescott against coming and he came anyway in the line of duty. There can be but one conclusion from the evidence the witnesses will present—Prescott was willfully and maliciously killed according to a premeditated plan. It is murder in the first degree." Moody went on to say that officer Prescott was merely doing his duty when he was murdered. Prescott had a warrant of arrest for Banks' participation in stealing election ballots on February 20, 1933, from the Jackson County Courthouse in Medford.

Election Ballots Stolen

Banks had been one of the leaders in the theft of the ballots. Banks had been especially interested in the recount in the county sheriff's election in November 1932 because one of his protégées was Sheriff Schermerhorn. Banks needed Schermerhorn to protect him against a number of pending lawsuits. Banks knew Schermerhorn would be willing to delay serving warrants on him. Former sheriff Ralph Jennings claimed the election had been mismanaged because 381 write-in votes supporting him had been discarded for "technical errors." Jennings thought he had actually won. Schermerhorn had won a majority of the votes by 123. Jennings challenged the process and Judge Skipworth agreed with him. So a recount was scheduled.

The night before the recount Llewellyn Banks and Judge Fehl led a big anti-government political rally. While the rally was in progress someone broke into the vault in the courthouse basement and stole ten thousand ballots. The stolen ballots were variously buried, dropped in the Rogue River, or burned. A recount of the sheriff's election was impossible. Unless the crime was solved Schermerhorn would remain sheriff.

Robert Ruhl wrote an editorial that appeared in his *Medford Mail Tribune* on the evening of February 21,*"The courthouse was broken into, the vault was smashed and the ballots, cast for sheriff at the last election, were stolen!"*

Participants in the crime, pressured by police, admitted that Banks had organized the theft. The Jackson County Grand Jury issued a warrant for Banks' arrest.

The Trial Resumes

Prosecutor Moody maintained that Banks had lain in wait for Prescott, that Banks knew Prescott was coming and he knew that he had a warrant for his arrest. Then, when Prescott knocked on his door, Mrs. Banks opened it the width of the chain lock. It was at that time Banks took aim through the partly opened door, shooting the constable. According to Moody, this "clearly pointed to premeditation on his part."

The defense countered that Banks had a clear and respectable record until a barrage of frivolous suits and indictments defamed him. The defense continued, "Mr. Banks knew the fruit business and in California between 1910-1926 he had amassed a fortune. He was operating as an independent, buying fruit for cash. Then he came to Jackson County and bought orchard property. In 1929 he purchased the *Medford News*. Defendant Banks was not a newspaper editor. He denounced the packing association, bankers, and other big interests. Again he was brought into conflict. It grew in intensity, until it culminated in the tragedy of March 16th. When Banks shot through the nearly closed door, it was the gesture of a cornered creature defending his home." It was a "warning to marauders who were trying to force their way in. The bullet ricocheted off the corner of the door, glanced off Prescott's hand and entered his body." Banks was a crusader, according to the defense.

And, as for Mrs. Banks, the defense asserted, *"She is just a wife and mother who had no part in the affair. Her presence here would be ridiculous if it were not pathetic."*

After the opening statements were completed, there was a short recess. In the following transcription, occasionally edited for brevity, Judge Skipworth is referred to as "The Court."

"You may call your first witness." The states first witness was George R. Carter who was sworn in to tell "the whole truth and nothing but the truth."

The Court: *Now, Mr. Carter, speak right up so we can hear you.*

Mr. Moody: *—speak so that the farthest juror may hear you without difficulty—. State you name.*

A. G.R. Carter.

Q. Where do you reside?

A. Medford.

Q. Do you occupy any official position in Jackson County?

A. County Clerk.

Q. Have you with you the original indictment that is returned by the grand jury of Jackson County and charging several defendants with burglary not in a dwelling?

A. I have.

(The reporter marks the paper indicated as State's Exhibit A for identification)

Q. I hand you State's Exhibit A for identification and will ask you to tell me what it is.

A. It is an indictment against Earl H. Fehl, Gordon Schermerhorn, John Glenn, J. Croft, and Thos. Brecheen, Chas. Davis, Walter J. Jones, J.A. La Dieu, Mason Sexton, Wilbur Sexton, C. Jean Conner, R.C. Cummings, Wesley Mcketrick, Virgil Edington, Claude Ward, Oliver Martin, L.A. Banks and others.

Q. Without reading it, what is it?

A. An indictment for larceny in a building not a dwelling.

Q. What date?

A. The 15th of March 1933.

At this point Mr. Moody asks the court and defense if he may read the indictment. Given permission he read the indictment concerning the above persons to- wit: "are accused by the Grand Jury of the County of Jackson by this Indictment of the crime of burglary not in a dwelling committed as follows: — did then and there willfully, unlawfully and feloniously break and enter a certain building, to-wit: The Jackson County Court House, the said above persons to commit larceny and steal therein by forcibly breaking an outer window of such building, contrary to the statutes in such cases made and provided, and against the peace and dignity of the State of Oregon."

Dated at Medford, Oregon in the County aforesaid, this 15th day of March, A.D. 1933. G.A. Codding, District Attorney.

Mr. Moody: *Q. Were the bench warrants issued as ordered?*

A. To the Constable George Prescott.

Q. Do you know how long he was constable of the Medford justice precinct?

A. From November 1924, on continuously.

After the cross-examination by defense attorney Lonergan, the witness was excused. The next state witness was sworn in.

Mr. Moody: *Now, speak loud so that the jury in the farthest seat may hear as well as The Court and counsel. State your name.*

A. Paul B. Rynning.

Q. Where do you live?

A. Medford, Oregon

Q. What business or occupation do you follow?

A. I am a civil engineer.

Q. I will ask you whether you made any drawing—or first I will ask you, do you know where the residence of Llewellyn A. Banks and his wife was in Medford during the month of March, 1933, and particularly the 16th day of March, 1933?

A. I do.

Q. Where?

A. 1000 East Main street---no, West Main street.

Q. West Main Street and what?

A. It is Peach Street.

Q. What kind of dwelling is it?

A. It is a one-story dwelling, with a very large porch on it, a number of rooms, and a basement.

Q. Did you make a drawing of the floor space of the first floor or the living part of the house?

A. I did.

The Court: *Mark the plat, Exhibit I for identification.*

Q. And it correctly produces the description and plan of the floor in that house, does it?

A. It does.

(After overruling objections from the defense the COURT received the map.)

The Court: *Mark it Exhibit 1. Let me see the map again after it is marked.*

The Court: *Q. The map is drawn to scale, is it?*

A. Yes, sir.

The Court: *Q. And from actual measurements taken by you?*

A. Yes, sir. One inch equals five feet.

The Court: *It will be received.*

(State's Exhibit 1, the map referred to, is placed on a blackboard in the view of the jury, Court and counsel)

The witness was cross-examined by defense counsel Mr. Lonergan. Afterwards the witness was excused.

The Court: *It is practically five o'clock. The audience will remain seated. Ladies and Gentlemen of the Jury, it is now five o'clock and we will take a recess until tomorrow morning at nine o'clock. Bear in mind the instruction I have heretofore given you not to talk about the case or read about it. Be here promptly tomorrow morning at nine-thirty o'clock. The audience will remain perfectly quiet until the jury passes out in charge of the bailiffs.*

May 4, 1933

Marian Lowry, reporter for the *Register Guard*, wrote about the spectators in the crowded courtroom that morning. One commented, "Just try and get six women agreed on a verdict of guilty for that man." And "two women sat on the front row of the spectators' section calmly working at their embroidery as they listened to testimony." And "Herb Owen could not stage a wrestling match with more gum-chewing specialists (especially of the feminine variety) than are seen at the Banks' trial."

Outside, it was another cloudy rainy day. At 9:30 am and the State's case resumed.

The State's first witness was Vern Shangle.

Q. And your name?

A. Vern Shangle.

Q. And what may be your occupation?

A. I am a photographer.

Q. How long have you been engaged in photography?

25

A. About twelve years.

Q. The taking of pictures and their development?

A. Yes.

Q. At whose instance were those photographs?

A. The county coroner Frank Pearl.

Q. I hand you State's Exhibits for identification J to O, both inclusive, and ask you to please state what they are.

A. This—

Q. Don't say "this."

The Court: *Refer to it as exhibit, whatever it may be.*

A. Exhibit J shows the door from the outside, closed; shows the bullet and the blood marks and the house number.

Mr. Moody: *The State offers in evidence, State's Exhibit J for identification.*

The Court: *Any objection?*

Photo showing exterior of front door with blood on the floor and bullet hole in edge of door
Photo from the Oregon State Archives collection

Mr. Lonergan: That is objected to, your Honor, on the ground that it is incompetent, irrelevant and immaterial and not within any of the issues of the case and it doesn't tend to prove any of the material elements of the indictment. It contains a typewritten statement on the back of the photograph that is wholly incompetent for any purpose for this case. It is not in any way binding upon these defendants or either of them and---

The Court: Well now, Mr. Lonergan, under the case of State vs. Clark, the photograph is competent so that the jury may understand the situation. In other words, it is the same as a map.

Mr. Lonergan: I understand that.

The Court: But this writing here on the back must be eliminated, else it cannot go to the jury.

Mr. Lonergan: I would like further at this time to urge the additional objection that it is incompetent and any other evidence introduced in the case is incompetent for the reason and the ground that there is no competent officer in charge of the prosecution of the case. There is no representative of the district attorney's office of Lane County engaged in this prosecution; therefore the entire prosecution is illegal.

The Court: The objection will be overruled.

Mr. Moody: (asks witness) Will you look at it and pass it on? Now, tear off any writing upon the back of any other of those exhibits.

(The witness removes some paper from the back of photographs)

Then a series of routine photographs of the interior and exterior were presented to the court by the State. Most were received as evidence.

Q. I am handing you State's Exhibit Z for identification and I will ask you in my examination not to state what the object photographed is but state whether you took that photograph.

A. Yes, I did.

(The exhibit referred to by counsel is handed to the court)

The Court: *(In a low tone out of hearing of the jury) Don't let the Jury see that.*

Mr. Moody: *Q. I am handing you State's Exhibit A-1 for identification and will ask you not to state what the object is that is photographed, but state whether or not you took that photograph and when. (Handing exhibit to witness.)*

A. Yes, I did. I made it at 11 am—March 16, 1933.

The Court: *(In low tone) Keep this from the jury.*

Mr. Moody: *All right, your Honor, I am not offering them at present.*

Q. I hand you State's Exhibit marked for identification A-2 and will ask you not to state what the object is but the date that you took the photograph.

A. March 16, 1933.

Q. I'm handing you State's Exhibit A-3 marked for identification and ask you not to state what the objects of the photograph is but whether or not you took it and when.

A. Yes I did, on March 16th 1933.

Despite the Judge's attempt to keep the corpse photographs from the jury and spectators when he whispered in a low voice "keep this from the jury," *Register-Guard* reporter Marian Lowry wrote, "They are pictures of the body of Constable George J. Prescott as it lay on the porch of the spacious Medford mansion of Llewellyn Banks, tried here for first degree murder. The spectators knew they were such pictures, so did everyone else."

After Mr. Moody finished with the photographer, Mr. Lonergan cross-examined him. When Lonergan finished his cross-examination the witness was excused.

The Court: *We will take a recess. The audience will remain seated until the jury passes out.*

Close up of Prescott's dead body showing upper torso and false teeth.
Photos from the Oregon State Archives collection

Dead body on porch
Photo from the Oregon State Archives

When the trial resumed, rain was pounding on the courthouse roof. Inside, every available seat was taken. People mingled outside the closed doors, waiting for someone to leave. One of the State's star witnesses was next. E.A. Fleming advanced to the witness stand. One reporter noted that Banks "eyed him sharply" and rocked nervously on his chair.

Q. State your name, please.

A. E.A. Fleming.

Q. Do you object to stating your age?

A. Sixty-seven.

Q. Where do you reside?

A. Jacksonville, Oregon.

Q. And what may be your occupation?

A. Orchardist.

Q. When you got to Medford where did you go?

A. I went to Mr. Banks'.

Q. What time did you arrive at Mr. Bank's residence?

A. Well, I would judge it was about fifteen minutes of ten or maybe a little later.

Q. And did you enter Mr. Banks' residence?

A. I did. I would say the east side, and the east side of the house. (Indicating on State's Exhibit l)

Q. Yes. Who admitted you?

A. Mr. Banks.

Q. Was there anyone else there?

A. Mrs. Banks was there and there were two others I think at that time, Mrs. Gutch and her husband.

Q. Did these two other parties, Mr. and Mrs. Gutch remain there while you were there?

A. Shortly after I went in the house they went out at the front door.

Q. And where was Mrs. Banks at this time?

A. In her domestic work.

Q. Now, how did you happen to go to Mr. Banks' residence that morning?

A. Why, to raise funds.

Q. It was a fund to defend the proceedings that had arisen over the ballot theft?

A. Yes, sir.

What Fleming is referring to was the Good Government Congress, an organization founded in January 1933 by Llewellyn Banks to confront the organized government of Jackson County.

Q. I wish you would just relate as near as you can in the exact words, if you can, the substance of them, of what you and Mr. Banks talked about. Say what you said and what he said.

A. After we had talked a few minutes about other things, Mr. Banks says, "They are fixing to make me the goat of the ballot proposition." I said, "Why?" Well, he says, "Mr. Coleman and Fehl were pocketed or closeted yesterday for two hours and they are fixing a political flop and they are going to make me the goat." Well, he says, "They can't do it, for I know nothing about it." And he says then, "No man can come up here with their trumped up warrants and serve on me for I will not go."

Q. Go on.

A. And then he said, "They will take me out feet first." And I says, "Mr. Banks, don't do that, oh, don't do that, it will get you in trouble. Then after I said that he said, "I will do it; I have said I will do it and no man can come through that door and take me." He says, "They will take me over their dead bodies, feet first." That's as near the language that I can remember he said at that time.

Q. How was Mr. Banks' demeanor that morning?

A. Very calm, no excitement; he didn't seem at all excited in any way.

Q. Well then, what happened?

A. The next word or next after that was I think that there came a rap on the door, "Mrs. Banks, you see who it is." And she says, "It is the officers."

Q. And what did Mr. Banks say then?

A. "You take those letters as you go and hand them to the officers."

Q. What did Mrs. Banks do then?

A. Well then, Mr. Banks says to me, "You better –you go". I picked up my overcoat then and started out the back way and Mrs. Banks started for the door, as near as I can remember the way it was now.

Q. Did you see Mrs. Banks open the door?

A. Yes, sir. Mrs. Banks says if I remember rightly, she says, "Here is two letters for you."

Q. Did you see who they were?

A. I did, one of them.

Q. Who was that?

A. That was Mr. Prescott.

Q. You were well acquainted with Mr. Prescott?

A. Yes, sir.

Q. Did you see anybody else?

A. Yes, I seen the top of his head.

Q. Who was it?

A. It was Jimmy O'Brien.

Q. That's Officer O'Brien of the state police?

A. Yes, sir.

Q. State how you went out so the record will show.

A. Went right on out through to this porch and down here and walked into the hands of Officer Warren.

Q. And he detained you?

A. Yes sir, he arrested me.

Fleming's country vernacular drew some laughter from the crowd. One newspaper article had him saying in reference to his speedy departure, "Brother, I thought it was the longest house I had ever been in."

The Court: *Have order in the courtroom. No demonstration whatever.*

Q. Now, after Mr. Banks told you to get out, did you see or hear anything?

A. As I walked out through the rooms and I got through the dining room or right about at the dining room I heard someone say, "Get Out," or "Look Out," in rather a loud voice. I could hear it plain and almost simultaneously (witness claps his hands) I supposed it was the blast from the gun.

Q. What did you do then?

A. I kept going.

The Court: *Have order in this courtroom, Mr. Bailiff I want you to keep order. This is no laughing matter at all.*

Q. Well, then you went on out?

A. Yes, sir.

Mr. Moody: *You may inquire.*

The Court: *Mr. Lonergan; it is so near the noon hour; rather than break into your cross-examination I think it better to adjourn.*

Mr. Lonergan: *Yes, your Honor.*

After the recess witness E.A. Fleming is recalled to the witness stand for cross-examination.

The Court: *I want to say to the audience, I want you to remain quiet. You know this is serious business we are engaged in and unless the audience is perfectly quiet, it is very difficult to carry on our court procedure in the manner in which it should be carried on. You will just please be as quiet as possible. You may proceed with the cross-examination.*

Q. You came from Medford. Where are you stopping?

A. Here in Eugene, in the jail.

The Court: *Have order now. What did I tell you? I will clear the courtroom.*

Q. How long have you been in jail?

A. Since the day that Mr. Prescott was killed.

Q. And you came to Eugene when?

A. Last Thursday.

Q. A week ago today?

A. Yes, sir.

Q. Mr. Fleming, you spoke this morning in direct-examination with reference to going to the home of Mr. and Mrs. Banks on the morning of the 16th of March, and you stated that you were conversing with Mr. Banks concerning the Good Government Congress, is that right?

A. Yes, sir.

Q. What is the Good Government Congress?

The Court: *Wait a minute until that car passes. Just pause a moment until it gets under way. (Loud car noise outside)*

A. It is a patriotic organization for the welfare of the community in general. It was supposed to be.

34

Q. Of what community?

A. Our immediate community in Jackson County.

Q. It was a county organization?

A. Well, I guess a county organization. They had units all over the county, at Jacksonville and over on the Applegate, and up at Trail, and all those places.

Q. What was the membership of this congress?

A. It was about six thousand.

Q. Were there fruit growers in the Good Government Congress?

A. Yes sir, plenty of them.

Q. It was not an organization limited then to the City of Medford alone?

A. Oh no, it was not by any means.

Q. How many units did they have in the county?

A. Oh, there must be around twenty units.

Q. And the purpose that you had in mind when you went to the Banks' home as I understand it was to have representatives of these different units to meet in order to formulate plans to defend the men who had been indicted on what was called the theft of the ballot case?

A. Yes, sir. In order to defray--- to raise money to defray the expense of this suit in defense of these boys.

Q. That was I suppose towards the purpose of hiring lawyers?

A. Yes, sir.

Q. Mr. Banks, Mr. Llewellyn A. Banks, one of the defendants in this case, was a member of the Good Government Congress?

A. Yes, sir.

Q. Did Mr. Banks hold any office in it that you know of?

A. I think honorary president.

Q. Who was the president?

A. Mrs. Henrietta Martin.

The lengthy cross-examination disclosed more members of the Good Government Congress, those involved with the ballot theft, a review of how Fleming exited the house, and how he was arrested. Mr. Fleming was then excused. Another witness, Mr. Earl Bryant, confirmed driving Fleming to Banks' home, and then he was excused. Then came state's witness James O'Brien under direct-examination by Mr. Moody.

Q. State you name in full.

A. James O'Brien.

Q. What is you occupation?

A. State police officer.

Q. Do you know Mr. Prescott?

A. I do. He was constable and city traffic officer of Medford.

Q. Did you meet him on the morning of March 16th, 1933?

A. Yes I did.

Q. Where?

A. At the state police office at Medford.

Q. What time did you meet him?

A. Eight-thirty.

Q. And where did you go?

A. Well, we started out to serve some warrants that we had that morning. The first place we went was out to Mr. Earl Fehl's place. That's the county judge of Medford.

Q. And from there?

A. We returned to the police office, and then to the Jackson Hotel and from there to Mr. Llewellyn A. Banks' home.

Q. Anybody else go with you?

A. Sergeants Warren and Lumsden followed us in another car.

Q. And when you got to Mr. Banks' residence relate what took place in your own language.

A. Well, we went up on the porch to serve the warrant on Mr. Banks and I knocked at the door with a little knocker that hangs on the door. We waited a little bit; there was some noise inside. I don't know what it was. Mrs. Banks came to the door and she opened the door and asked, "What is it?" Mr. Prescott says, "I have a warrant here for Mr. Banks' arrest." And then she began closing the door and as she did Mr. Prescott put his foot on the threshold and he said, "Just a minute, I will read it" or "Let you read it." I don't remember exactly which it was, and I had been watching through the door during this time which was very short, and I saw Mr. Banks appear in the room there or in the dining room right between the two rooms and he had this rifle leveled to his shoulder

The steps leading up to the front door. *Photo from the Oregon State Archives.*

and he called out, "Look out", and I cried, "Look out, George." At the same instant, and I stepped back below the range of the glass. There was a small glass window in the upper section of the door. I stepped back below that and grabbed him and tried to pull him then and push him away.

Q. Tried to pull him? Who?

A. Mr. Prescott. And just as I did so, the shot was fired. And it apparently hit Mr. Prescott in the hand first because there was an explosion there right in my face and there was particles of the flesh flew from his hand, and bone also, and I got some particles of slivers in my eye, and trying to get him away from the door just at that instant, and I lost my balance and Mr. Prescott did also and of course his teeth dropped from in front just the minute he was hit. He had false teeth and they closed down over his mouth and he fell backwards and I somewhat lost my hold on him until after he had hit the floor but I did have a hold of the coat sleeve of this arm that was hit. (Witness indicating) And I jumped up again and I just got a glance of the man standing in the room there with the rifle and apparently making some movement and then a man running from the room attracted my vision. That man later proved to be Mr. Fleming. And from there I run across the porch, the west side. The door was closed and that latch was solid. I tried that. I run across to the west side of the porch and vaulted over that edge of the porch there and as I passed that window I saw Mrs. Banks right in the line with the fireplace. I couldn't see anything until I got beyond that, and I vaulted over the west side of the porch and I squatted down behind the porch there and I waited some time, possibly a minute or a minute and a quarter. I couldn't tell you exactly. And then I left there and went over towards the hedge and was going to walk to the house across the street and I thought I had better get in the car and I came back to the car which was parked directly in front and I drove the car around to an apartment house which is on the next street west of the Mr. Banks' residence. I went in there and I stepped out in front and I watched the residence for a moment and then I went in there and telephoned, and after I came out I looked at the residence again and got in the car and

38

drove through the alley to inform Sergeants Warren and Lumsden what had happened, and I drove through the alley and Mr. Lumsden was standing parallel with the west side of the house by a telephone pole and Mr. Warren was standing right near the garage parallel to the east side of the house and he had Mr. Fleming in custody then, and as I went through there I stopped for a moment and told them what had transpired and that I had called headquarters for reinforcements and was going to throw a gas bomb in the house to force them out after the reinforcements arrived and I was going –

Mr. Lonergan: *If your Honor please, I move to strike out the answer of the witness on the ground that it is wholly incompetent, irrelevant and immaterial what he was going to do, going to throw a gas bomb in there, I move that be stricken from the record.*

The Court: *Yes, the answer of the witness that he was going to throw a gas bomb in the house to force them out is stricken out. The jury will disregard it. State what you actually did.*

A. From where Sergeants Warren and Lumsden were standing at the rear of the house I drove on Peach Street across Main and took up a point of observation over there. I waited until reinforcements arrived, and as they did Mr. McCredie and Lieutenant Dunn of the state police department were the first to arrive, my eye was bothering me quite badly and I asked Mr. McCredie to remove the splinter from it. He took my handkerchief but he was too nervous, he couldn't do it, and Mr. Kelly, the attorney, was there, and he cleaned my eye out in fairly good shape, and I guess that was about all until Captain Bown arrived then shortly afterwards. I had gone back to the west side of the house and Captain Bown came out and I was standing there and Mr. Love accompanied him. They come out and they got out of the car and they went up towards the porch. I couldn't see them go on the porch from where I was. Well, then they returned again and they had Mr. Banks in custody, and after they left with Mr. Banks I went up on the porch and the coroner was there and instructed Mr. Shangle, a photographer, who had arrived, to take some pictures of the body in its posi-

tion, and such as that, and then to come in the house and to take pictures within the house. I knocked on the door and as I knocked on the door I saw Mrs. Banks sitting way back in the back part of the dining room. That's the north end of the living room. I knocked a couple of times and she came to the door and at first she asked what I wanted, and I told her who I was and that we wanted to pick up any articles of evidentiary value that was in the place.

The Court: *Pick up what? Hold on a minute. Mr. Bailiff, I wish you would go over and see if you can find out what is the matter with that dog and if possible silence it. (A dog was making a ruckus outside.)*

A. Pick up any articles of evidentiary value that was in the place, and we looked the place over. After Mrs. Banks let us in we talked a few minutes and she told us where Mr. Banks had stood when he fired the shot.

Mr. Moody: *Now, where did she say that he stood? Take that plat, State's Exhibit 1, and point out where Mrs. Banks stood and Mr. Banks stood.*

Mr. Lonergan: *That is objected to, your Honor, on the ground that it is incompetent, irrelevant and immaterial, a statement not made in the presence of the defendant, Llewellyn A. Banks and therefore cannot be binding on him in any way.*

The Court: *Wouldn't it be competent as to Mrs. Banks?*

Mr. Lonergan: *If at all, that would be its only purpose of course.*

The Court: *Yes, unless Mr. Banks was present at the time it wouldn't be binding on him, but it would be binding on Mrs. Banks.*

Mr. Moody: *Now, stand over that way so as to not have your back between the plat and the jury and point out to the jury where Mrs. Banks said Mr. Banks stood when he fired the shot.*

A. She pointed to a point about in there. (Witness indicating on State's Exhibit 1)

The Court: *Make a circle there, and put your initials.*

40

Mr. Moody: *Now, what else did Mrs. Banks say?*

A. She then—we asked her if that was the rifle, referring to a rifle setting on the table, that he used, and she told us that it was.

The Court: *Examine it and see whether it is empty or not and don't point it towards me.*

(A rifle is handed to the witness)

A. There is no shell in the chamber, no bullet in the chamber.

Mr. Moody: *State what in the way of weapons, if any, did you find there in the house.*

A. I found this rifle that I have here in my hand. And a forty-four Smith and Wesson revolver in a holster and –attached to a cartridge belt.

Mr. Lonergan: *I would suggest that he take them out.*

The Court: *Very well. If the revolver is loaded, the shells should be ejected.*

The rifle on table,
Photo from the Southern Oregon Historical Society collection

Mr. Moody: If the Court pleases, I want the record to show that they were loaded when found.

The Court: That will be all right. You can prove that.

Mr. Moody: I will ask you if the pistol that you saw there was loaded:

A. It was, yes.

Mr. Moody: I want someone here that knows how to unload a pistol.

Mr. Lonergan: I know how to empty it.

Mr. Moody: I will get away from you while you are doing it.

(Mr. Lonergan ejects the shells from the revolver.)

The Court: Let the shells be marked A-6.

Mr. Moody: I hand you State's Exhibits D-H for identification and ask you if you have ever seen them before.

A. These are some of the warrants that we were serving that morning.

Q. And did he have these warrants in his pocket at the time that he was shot?

A. Yes, he did.

The newspaper reporters and spectators could see that officer Prescott's blood had been splattered on the warrants he was attempting to serve.

Q. Do you know who shot Prescott?

A. I do, yes.

Q. Who?

A. Mr. Llewellyn A. Banks.

There was a short recess and James O'Brien was called back to the witness stand. "Just two Irishmen locking horns" was the comment from one spectator as Lonergan cross-examined James O'Brien.

Q. When was the first time that you saw the warrants? Did you see them on the 15th of March?

A. Yes, I did, on the night of the 15th.

Q. What?

A. On the night of the 15th.

Q. Where did you see them on the night of the 15th?

A. Well, we served two warrants on that night.

Q. Was there any attempt made to serve Mr. Banks on the evening of the 15th of March?

A. No, there was not.

Q. Who was the first that the warrant was served upon on the evening of the 15th of March?

A. It was served on Arthur La Dieu.

Q. And whom else did you serve that evening, or did Mr. Prescott serve?

A. We served another one on John Glenn at Ashland.

Q. And when was the warrant served on Judge Fehl?

A. It was served on him about a week later.

Q. He was right there in the city, of course, Medford?

A. If he was we didn't know it. We were searching for him and had information that he was hiding at Grants Pass and various other places, but he was not in town, because we were looking for him, that is, that we could find out.

Q. You had his house surrounded there, didn't you?

A. No, we did not.

43

Q. What?

A. We did not.

Q. You mean you--- The house was surrounded, was it not?

A. Not that I had any knowledge of.

Q. Now, as I understand it there was no attempt at all to serve a warrant on Mr. Banks on the evening of March 15th?

A. No.

Q. And the first visit that was made to his house for the purpose of serving a warrant was on the morning of the 16th of March?

A. Yes.

Q. At which time you and Mr. Prescott drove there in a state police car, is that correct?

A. Yes.

Q. And two detectives of the state police went in another car and came in the back way of the premises, that's correct, isn't it?

A. Yes.

Q. Now, when you went to the Banks home on the morning of the 16th of March in company with Mr. Prescott, who was carrying the warrants?

A. Mr. Prescott.

Q. Where did he have them?

A. He had them in his inside coat pocket.

Q. Well, just how do you know that now?

A. Because I just glanced at him like that (indicating) and saw him take the warrants out of his pocket this way, reaching in for them. (Indicating)

Q. You mean you saw him reaching into his pocket?

A. I saw him with his coat pulled back and he had the warrants in about this position, I should say. (Indicating) He had his hand on them. I do know that.

Mr. Moody: *Will you state that in the record so that the record will be clear.*

Mr. Lonergan: *And they were not withdrawn from his pocket?*

A. Presumably not.

Q. Presumably? Well, were they or were they not? You claim you were there?

A. No, they were not, not that I saw.

Q. He didn't take his overcoat off did he?

A. No.

Q. You were standing alongside of Mr. Prescott, were you?

A. Yes, I was.

Q. And on which side of him were you as you approached the door there?

A. I was standing on his left side.

Q. And that's the same position that you maintained relatively during the entire time that it took for this occurrence to transpire, wasn't it?

A. Yes, sir.

Q. Now, when you went to the Banks home and got up to the door, the front door on the south side of the house, you used the knocker, as I understand it, to announce your arrival?

A. Yes.

Q. And which one was it that used the knocker?

A. It was myself.

Q. And in response to that the door was opened slightly?

A. Yes.

Q. When the door was opened you saw that it was on a chain, did you not?

A. No, I really didn't notice the chain at that time.

Q. And when the door was opened Mr. Prescott put his foot in it quickly didn't he?

A. When she started to close the door, yes.

Q. Well, the door was only opened a very few inches, wasn't it?

A. Yes.

Q. So that if she had started to close the door, and made any movement toward that at all he wouldn't have had room to put his foot in there, would he?

A. Yes. He was looking for such an act, I suppose.

Q. Well, you are supposing now? You are supposing, aren't you?

A. Yes.

Mr. Lonergan: *Well, I move that the supposition be stricken from the record.*

The Court: *That statement that "I suppose he was looking for such act, I suppose" is stricken out. The jury will disregard it.*

Mr. Lonergan: *The fact of the matter is he did put his foot in there in the space left by reason of opening of the door?*

A. Yes.

Q. And put his shoulder against the door?

A. No.

Q. Isn't it a fact now that both you and he were pushing on that door to force it open?

A. Absolutely not.

Q. And when he stood up there before the door which foot did he put in the opening?

A. He put his left foot in the opening.

Q. He put his left foot in. I see. I am directing your attention to the plat, marked State's Exhibit 1, and directing your attention to what has been described here as the south and main entrance to the Banks home. This is the place where you and Mr. Prescott appeared before the house of Mr. Banks, is that correct?

A. Yes.

Q. And which way does that door open?

A. It opens in.

Q. And when the door was slightly opened, as you estimate it about five inches, I believe you said yesterday, is that correct?

A. Yes, sir.

Q. Mr. Prescott stuck his left foot in there?

A. Well, he put his foot in there to hold the door open.

Q. I know what he put his foot in there for, but you said he put his foot in there?

A. Yes, sir.

Q. Well, did he or didn't he?

A. He did, yes. If you are referring to putting his foot in the entire opening--

Q. I am referring to nothing. I am taking your story now for the present. I am not a witness here. I am just taking your statement. Now, when you went up to the door of the Banks home and used the knocker to attract attention, I believe you testified on direct-examination that the first one you saw, looking through the window there, was Mrs. Banks?

A. No, I didn't see Mrs. Banks when I was looking through the window.

Q. Where did you see her, and how, if at all?

A. I saw her through the opening of the door.

Q. You saw no one then in the Banks home at all until the door was opened partly?

A. No.

Q. And at that time you saw Mrs. Banks as she opened the door and stood there in the four or five inch opening?

A. Yes.

Q. What did she say?

A. The only thing I remember her saying was "What is it?" or "What do you want?" That's all I can remember her saying.

Q. And was there any reply made to her?

A. Yes.

Q. By whom?

A. By Mr. Prescott.

Q. What did he say?

A. He said he had a warrant for Mr. Banks' arrest.

Q. Now, when did you if at all see Mr. Banks in the house?

A. I saw Mr. Banks just an instant before the shot was fired.

Q. Mr. Banks called out you think, to "look out", or to "get out'?

A. "Look out".

From here in the trial Mr. Lonergan tried his best to make O'Brien look clumsy as a police detective by insinuating that his notebook writings were unorganized. He used a sarcastic voice in describing Officer O'Brien's lack of knowledge on different types of lace and silk that was used as a window covering on the glass window in the door. But officer O'Brien was resolute in his answers, even at times getting the upper hand in the questioning. The cross-examination got tougher, so much so that the States attorney had to caution Mr. Lonergan.

Mr. Moody declared: *"Treat the witness respectfully."*

Mr. Lonergan: *Well, I am.*

The Court: *Hold on. Go ahead with your examination.*

Mr. Lonergan: *I don't like to be criticized by counsel, your Honor.*

The Court: *Well, counsels say things sometimes in the heat of trial they don't really mean. Go ahead. You are within your rights. Go ahead.*

In another exchange of tense emotions Mr. Lonergan accused O'Brien of deliberately staging a scene for the coroner's photographer. Near the front room a photograph had been taken of a card table with the rifle, revolver and cartridge belt on it. O'Brien had testified, under direct-examination that that was how he had found them when he entered the room. On cross- examination things took a savage turn:

Q. You were in the house then alone, weren't you, with her?

A. No, I was not. I didn't go in alone.

Q. Who was with you?

A. Sergeant Warren.

Q. Oh, one of your police officers?

A. Yes.

Q. But there was no one with Mrs. Banks?

A. Yes.

Q. Isn't it a fact when you came into that house and Mrs. Banks was there alone, Mr. Banks having been taken away, that you put the revolver and the cartridge belt over there on the same table with the rifle and held it there until the picture was taken?

A. I did no such thing in any manner whatever.

A *Register Guard* reporter heard it this way: "It most certainly was nothing of the sort!" Replied O'Brien heatedly, "I had nothing to do with the weapons except to see them as *I entered the room.* "

May 5, 1933

Among the spectators crowding the courtroom Friday morning were Dean Roy Hewitt of Willamette University law school, Salem; C.M. Green, Manager of the *Ashland Tidings*, newspaper; and A.E. Wheeler, one of Eugene's oldest lawyers. The prominent men, and the rest of the spectators, had undoubtedly come to see more than just a murder trial. They were hoping to learn about the rebellion that had spread in Jackson County for the last two years. Judge Skipworth however seemed intent on keeping the trial focused on the murder of Prescott. He knew that a separate trial would handle the ballot box theft.

The morning started with Lonergan's cross-examination of Officer O'Brien. The defense made sarcastic remarks again about the officer's logbook. Then he dismissed the witness.

The prosecution then called its next witness, Colonel E.E. Kelley.

Mr. Moody: Where do you reside:

A. Medford, Oregon.

Q. How long have you lived there?

A. Since 1907.

Q. What is you occupation?

A. I'm a lawyer.

Q. Were you acquainted with Constable George Prescott?

A. I was.

Q. At the time that you had got there had Mr. Banks been arrested?

A. He had not.

Q. And how soon after you got there was he taken in custody?

A. It might have been five or ten minutes. That is when he came out of the front door of the residence and went through the crowd that had gathered and was taken in an automobile.

Q. Did you go up to the porch?

A. I did.

Q. Well, what did you see when you got on the porch?

A. I saw the body of George Prescott lying on the floor of the porch. He was lying on his back with his left hand up on his chest.

Q. Was he alive or dead?

A. He was dead.

Q. Describe that door.

A. The bullet had caught the door in the edge, splintering veneered pieces of wood off the outside.

Q. Did you notice anything on the door on the outside?

A. On the right hand casing, there was blood spattered over the casing and some on the door.

Q. Do you know Officer James O'Brien?

A. Yes. I saw him before Mr. Banks came out of the house. It was just as soon as I arrived out there that I saw Officer O'Brien. He was suffering from an inflammation of the right eye, and I took a handkerchief and took two pieces of what appeared to be little slivers of wood out of his eye. One of them was in the white of the eye, and the other was on the inside angle of the eye, two apparent slivers of wood. And his face was splattered with blood at the time and I tried to wash that off.

Q. Now, are you familiar with firearms?

A. Yes, sir.

Q. I hand you State's Exhibit A-4 and ask you what kind of a gun that is?

A. I think that is a Newton hunting rifle.

The Court: *Don't point it at me.*

(One newspaper account of the incident said, "As he handled the gun, Colonel Kelly pointed it in several directions, which brought a reprimand from the judge.)

Mr. Moody: *I hand you State's Exhibit A-8 (cartridges that had previously been extracted from the rifle in court) and ask you to examine and tell us the character of those cartridges.*

A. Those are sporting cartridges. They're what is known as the mushrooming bullet.

Q. What is the difference in the shocking power?

A. Well, this bullet here when it encounters a bone in the body it mushrooms immediately, and it tears everything away in front of it. A man shot through the head, there would be a hole in the back of his head as big as your fist ordinarily. These bullets are discharged from a gun that is rifled and it has a rotating spinning motion when it goes out.

After a very short cross-examination by Mr. Lonergan the witness was excused.

The next state's witness was Doctor Benton C. Wilson. He had helped in the autopsy with a Doctor Drummond on the afternoon of March 16, 1933. He was asked to explain the nature of the wounds on Prescott's body. Dr. Wilson recounted that they first discovered a large wound in the officer's left hand. They had to pick out pieces of wood splinters. They then discovered a gaping hole, "about two inches in diameter" at the left shoulder with the wound continuing "down back and to the right." The third, second, and fourth ribs were splintered. The wound continued through the left lung, leaving about a quart of blood in the left cavity, and smashing the sixth rib next to the spinal cord in the back. They turned the body over and removed pieces of metal from the back. As part of the direct-examination both the judge and Mr. Moody had to remind the witness on several occasions to speak more clearly and louder. Near the end of the questioning Doctor Benton Wilson was asked:

Mr. Moody: From your examination of the body of Mr. Prescott can you state what caused his death?

A. Well, it was most certainly caused by the impact of some blunt object tearing tissues, causing shock and laceration and hemorrhage within the left chest.

With this information the court recessed for the noon hour. When court resumed the next prosecution witness was Frank Pearl, county coroner. He affirmed what Wilson had said. Following him was undertaker H.W. Conger. Then came another star witness for the prosecution, Tommy E. Williams. Up until this point in the trial Edith Banks had hardly been mentioned. But during William's testimony under direct-examination by Mr. Moody this would change.

Q. Where do you reside?

A. Medford, Oregon, for ten years.

Q. What is you business?

A. Manager of Union Oil.

Q. On March 16, 1933, what were you doing between ten and half-past eleven that morning?

A. Driving the truck.

Q. Did you have occasion to drive by the Banks' residence that morning?

A. Yes, sir.

Q. Did anybody from the residence at any time that morning call you?

A. Mrs. Banks.

Q. What did she say to you and how did she call you? Did she hand you something? Or not?

A. She did. When I went up there I was looking straight at her when I went up on the porch and she had what I thought at the time, looking across the street, I thought it was a letter. Instead of that afterwards it turned out to be a blotter of cardboard and it was extended like this so I could read it. Then she said, "Will you take this to the state police?"

The Court: *Exhibit A-9, I think for identification.*

Mr. Moody: *Is this that card?*

A. That's the same card that was handed me.

Mr. Moody: *(Reading state's Exhibit A-9) "Come and get George Prescott and you will be all right. Then proceed in order. Mrs. Banks."*

Q. Did you have any conversation with her?

A. I did. I said, "Where is George:" And she nodded her head this way.

Q. And what did you do then?

A. I said, "Who killed him?" and she said, "We did; he tried to break into our home."

Q. And was that all of the conversation?

A. That was all of the conversation. Mrs. Banks closed the door.

The Court: *You have finished with your direct-examination?*

Mr. Moody: *Yes, you Honor.*

The Court: *Cross-examine.*

Mr. Lonergan began questioning Tommy Williams.

Q. You knew Mr. Prescott?

A. Very well. He was a wonderful man.

Q. When you asked where Prescott was, you say Mrs. Banks said what?

A. I said, "Where is George?" She nodded her head like this and I said, "Who killed him?" She said, "We did, he tried to break into our home."

Q. Where was the body at that time?

A. It was to the east of the door.

Q. It was right there in front of you, wasn't it?

A. It was east of the door approximately six feet.

The cross-examination continued until adjournment at 5pm. The cross-examination of Tommy Williams would continue on Saturday at 9:30 May 6, 1933.

The lead paragraph of Friday's *Medford Mail Tribune* referred to the testimony of Tommy Williams and noted that when asked who had killed Prescott Mrs. Banks had said, "We did it!" The prosecution had scored a point in proving that Mrs. Banks was complicit in the death of the Jackson county constable.

May 6, 1933.

Before the defense began its questioning of Mr. Williams the court along with prosecution and defense attorneys decided to adjourn the trial at noon. Judge Skipworth said, "There is a tremendous strain on everybody connected with the case and so a little rest may be an advantage."

Mr. Moody called the next prosecution witness, Mr. C.A. Warren from Gladstone, Oregon. Mr. Warren was Sergeant of investigations for the state police department.

Q. Were you in Medford on March 16, 1933?

A. I Was.

Q. Where did you meet Prescott?

A. He came to my room in the Jackson Hotel.

Q. Did he come alone?

A. He came in the company with Sergeant O'Brien of the state police department.

Q. Was there anybody else present in your room other than you three?

A. Sergeant Lumsden of the state police department.

Q. Where did you go?

A. Mr. Banks' residence.

(Warren and Lumsden had followed Prescott and O'Brien in another vehicle.)

Q. Did you see where Mr. O'Brien and Mr. Prescott went?

A. As we drove down west Main Street they were right immediately ahead of us, and we turned down Peach Street as they pulled in front of the Banks home. (Warren and Lumsden stationed themselves at the back of the house.)

Q. Did anything transpire while you were there?

A. I met Mr. Fleming there. He came out of the back door and started down the steps and I walked over and stopped him.

Q. Did you or did you not place Mr. Fleming under arrest?

A. I did.

Q. Where did you go after that?

A. I went into the Banks' home, through the front door.

Q. What room did you first enter?

A. I entered the living room.

Q. And who were there?

A. At the time, Sergeant Lumsden, Sergeant O'Brien and Mrs. Banks were in the room.

The testimony determined that Warren saw a card table in the hall with a rifle, revolver, holster for the revolver, and a cartridge belt on it. Warren went on to describe the room arrangement of the house and the other paraphernalia he found. In Banks' bedroom for example, he found a suitcase partly packed and containing, among other things, a quantity of ammunition. There were also outdoor clothes and high leather boots lying beside the suitcase. Mr. Warren's testimony took him back to the front room and the scene of the crime.

Q. Did you have any conversation with Mrs. Banks?

A. I did.

Q. What was that conversation?

Mr. Lonergan: *That is objected to, you Honor, on the ground that it is incompetent, irrelevant and immaterial and not within any of the issues of the case; and is in no way binding upon the defendant, Llewellyn A. Banks, unless he was present, and there is no showing that he was. On the further ground that it is an invasion of the constitutional rights of the defendant, Edith Banks, and that any statement she made was made without any warning or any statement by the officers as to her rights and with out legal representation.*

The Court: *Well, it will be competent for the state to show any statements that Mrs. Banks made, provided they were made voluntarily and freely and without any hope of reward or under duress, and furthermore it would not be competent as to the defendant, Llewellyn A. Banks, but only as to Mrs. Banks herself, and it will be limited to that purpose. Provided you lay the foundation.*

Mr. Moody: *Was Mrs. Banks' statement voluntary?*

A. It was.

Q. It was not made under any stress or threat?

A. It was not.

Q. And without any promise or hope of reward?

A. There was none.

Q. You may now state what---

A. I asked Mrs. Banks what had happened. She told me a knock came on the door. That she had gone to the door and had informed Mr. Banks that George Prescott was at the door. She stated that Mr. Banks instructed her to get those letters, which were lying on the table, and deliver them to Mr. Prescott. I asked her what those letters were and she stated that Mr. Banks had dictated to her the letters in the morning, one addressed to chief of police McCready and the other to Captain Lee Bown of the state police. She stated that in those letters he had instructed him not to send an officer there.

Mr. Moody: *Go ahead.*

A. She went to the door and at that time the chain was hanging down. I asked her to show me just what had happened. She placed the burglary chain in place and opened the door and showed how

The inside of the house
Photo from the OregonState Archives

she stood at the door and opened the door, and that she had hand-
ed the letters out to Prescott and asked him to please go away and
that at that time Mr. Prescott had attempted to break in and "we
had to shoot him. That was her statement at that time.

On cross-examination Mr. Lonergan asked if Warren had a
search warrant. They had none. Mr. Lonergan's questioning lasted
until noon. Then the court was adjourned until Monday morning at
9:30 a.m.

Ruhl vs. KKK

In March 1909, editor George Putnam of the *Medford Tribune* wrote: The paper that has no enemies has no friends... The *Tribune* has critics—but "to escape criticism, say nothing, do nothing, be nothing, and the *Tribune* has something to say, something to do, and intends always to be a vital force in the life of the community. It has the courage of its convictions."

George Putnam was an experienced editor before coming to Medford in 1906, at the age of 38. He had already been a reporter for the *San Diego Tribune*, founder and editor of the *Spokane Press*, editor of the *Eureka Herald*, and news editor of the *Oregon Journal*.

In 1907 Mr. Putnam witnessed an assault on Medford's mayor. The President of the Rogue River Valley Railroad, W.S. Barnum had used an ax to attack Mayor J.F. Reddy. At trial Barnum got off scot-free. Enraged, George Putnam wrote an article critical of the jury and prosecution. He was indicted for libel in December 1907 and a warrant issued for his arrest. He was arrested in Douglas County and jailed in Roseburg. Following internment Putnam wrote editorials that exposed the jail for unsanitary conditions, "Unfit for habitation." Putnam returned to Jacksonville where he was tried and convicted in January 1908 and fined $150. He had given substantial journalistic rationale for his editorial, and his case was even supported by then railroad commissioner Oswald West, who would later become Oregon's governor. The case was appealed to the Oregon Supreme Court, where a new trial was ordered. At the new trial Putnam was exonerated.

Another highly talented editor, Robert Waldo Ruhl came to Medford in 1911. Ruhl made a substantial investment in the *Medford Sun* and *Medford Mail Tribune*. His new associates were Putnam and S. Sumpter Smith of the *Medford Sun*. Mr. Ruhl brought with him an esteemed reputation. In 1903 he had graduated from Harvard. Ruhl had worked on the Harvard newspaper *Crimson* alongside Franklin D. Roosevelt. After graduation Mr. Ruhl worked as a reporter for the *New York Globe* for four years. In 1907 he purchased an interest in the Rockford, Illinois *Daily Republic* and became its managing editor in 1908. From 1909 to 1910 he was the editorial writer for the *Spokesman Review* of Spokane, Washington. Then in 1910 he married Mable Works. They decided to settle down in Medford. Robert Ruhl was 31 years old.

What may have attracted the Ruhls to Jackson County was its astounding growth. From 1890 to 1910 the population had more than doubled from 11,455 to 25, 756. Seemingly endless economic opportunities abounded. Encompassing Medford was the Rogue River Valley with a mild climate perfect for agriculture. With the arrival of the Southern Pacific Railroad and commencement of construction on the Pacific Highway (the future Highway 99), getting farm products to the nation was much easier.

By 1914 the *Medford Mail Tribune* was touting the Medford area as one of the best farming and fruit growing places on the continent. At 1500 feet of elevation, with topography allowing the land to drain adequately, and with 27 inches of annual rainfall supplemented with new irrigation systems the land was ideal for apples and especially pears. Photographs from the era show pear trees laden with so much fruit, that the branches had to be propped up with two by four boards. Pear shipments increased from 125 railroad carloads in 1911 to 450 carloads in 1913. Cooperative fruit associations were formed to assist the farmers.

Testimonials from area farmers appeared in the January 1, 1914 issue of the *Medford Mail Tribune*. D.A. Wood wrote, "I must say with plenty of delicious fruit and fresh vegetables, pure water, and the productiveness of the soil in the way of crops, the mild climate and fine scenery, surely this is an ideal place to own a stock and dairy ranch, also for a home."

Manager, J.H. Randoph of Producers' Fruit Company, wrote, "The season has been ideal from a marketing standpoint, and notwithstanding the slump in Bartletts, which brought the pear averages down, I believe that general results are eminently satisfactory to everybody, and am in hopes that we may have another season just like it in 1914."

Along with the fruit industry, there was gold mining, grain farming, logging, road building and tourism. The Rogue River provided, some of the best fishing in the northwest, with 8-pound steelhead and trout.

The editors of the *Medford Mail Tribune* supported this economic growth, but they were also outspoken and tackled issues that affected the local people. In one editorial the editors denounced smoking especially for youth claiming it prevented normal development. In another they criticized unnecessary use of smudge pots, burning crude oil in open pots to prevent frost damage to fruit as "soot spreading contrivances."

In 1919 George Putnam decided to leave. He had invested heavily in the *Capital Journal* in Salem. So he sold his interests in the *Tribune* and *Medford Sun* to Robert Ruhl and Smith. Putnam summed up his service to the *Medford Daily* in a column.

"During all these years of boom, years of slump and years of recuperation—the *Mail Tribune* has been aggressively on the firing line for progress.

An indulgent public has apparently become convinced of my sincerity—for I have not been jailed or assaulted for a long time. Its toleration has earned it a respite—or some would say—a surcease of evil."

On April 2, 1919 Robert W. Ruhl wrote: "In short, to be as

brief and painless as possible, this paper is to be independent. Not independent in a non-partisan sense, but independent in a literal and perfectly sincere sense. Shocking, we know, but true, quite true."

This independent policy was considered visionary at the time. Papers were either Democratic or Republican. Editor Ruhl set about changing that rule. "As soon as the fog lifts and we can see what the parties are and what they stand for, we are going to back the one we like best and run on high till the end of the campaign…"

Robert Ruhl in his office at the *Medford Mail Tribune*
Photo from the Southern Oregon Historical Society collection

With this inspiring credo the *Mail Tribune* was launched into the 1920s. The First World War was over. The Southern Pacific railroad had sliced through the manufacturing districts of Medford, bringing new lumber mills, new canneries, and new storage houses. Irrigation canals channeled water to the fruit orchards, tripling production.

Two important contests were coming up in November 1922 general election: the governor's race and an initiative measure that would require all children to attend public schools. Known as the compulsory Education Bill, it would eliminate parochial schools of all kinds. The Scottish Rite Masons, and the KKK parties backed the bill because they disliked Catholics. The *Mail Tribune* wrote in June 1922 that secret bosses of the Masons and the KKK had met a year earlier to recruit apostate nuns and priests to make anti-parochial school presentations throughout Oregon. "The most lurid picture of the old fashioned Papist menace was painted." And just prior to the primary "every county in the state was flooded with printed pamphlets, charging the Catholic Church with every crime committed since the flood." By this time the KKK had gained a considerable foothold in Oregon, with chapters in Tillamook, Medford, Eugene, Portland and Ashland. They captured many local and county offices and even won a few seats in the state legislature.

The KKK suffered a setback in March 1922, when word spread that they had been behind three non-fatal hangings in Jackson County. Vigilantes in robes and masks had threatened a white man, a black man and a man of Mexican heritage. Two were even hoisted off the ground with the noose around their necks. All of them were harassed out of Oregon.

In Portland the Klan was becoming a political force. Community leaders there posed alongside hooded and gowned Klan representatives for publicity photographs. The mayor of Medford, Charles E. Gates accepted honorary membership into the Klan just prior to the May gubernatorial primary.

Governor Olcott feared the Invisible Empire was trying to usurp political control in Oregon. On May 13, 1922 he issued a proclamation: "Dangerous forces are insidiously gaining a foothold in Oregon. I call upon all loyal citizens of this state to give support to the proper law enforcing arms of the government in this movement against masked riders or cloaked and disguised figures who unlawfully skulk about on secret missions for unknown ends. These practices must cease!"

On the 16th of May the Medford City Council passed a new city ordinance: "No person shall wear upon any public street any mask, cap, cowl, hood or other thing concealing the identity of the wearer." The fine was up to $100 or imprisonment for thirty days.

Significantly, the Governor's attempt to face down the Ku Klux Klan was hurting his reelection campaign. The state Republican Party was about to elect its gubernatorial nominee. The two leading contenders were Olcott and state senator Charles Hall. Hall had endorsed the Compulsory Education Initiative backed by the Klan. In fact, it was his major campaign issue. Governor Olcott opposed it.

Robert Ruhl editorialized against the Klan in the *Medford Mail Tribune* and supported Governor Olcott. Ruhl kept tract of the KKKs operation in California and proudly saluted California's efforts to rid that state of the secret organization. He wrote:

With Olcott as the nominee the Republicans of the state can go to the polls united, with confidence and self-respect. Not only will this absurd attempt to foist an invisible empire of invisible buncombe on the state of Oregon be given its quietus once and for all, but the man best qualified for the position of governor will have been elected.

When the election narrowed down to a contest between free and open government on the one hand, and invisible government on the other, then this paper decided to enter the primary and do everything in its power to prevent this masked order from getting control of this county and state.

The so-called creed is essentially un-American and dangerous. The preposterous attempt to enter politics and capture the government is outrageous.

But first, last, and all the time, the KKK. is a joke. After one has studied it for any length of time, indignation evaporates and there is only one escape: Fresh air and a good laugh with puck: 'What Fools We Mortals Be!'

Despite Ruhl's editorial help, and perhaps because most other Oregon newspapers were silent on the KKK issue, Olcott barely squeaked by, winning by fewer then 100 votes statewide.

The Klan's power was growing throughout Oregon. The night skies were ablaze with the burning of crosses. The *Medford Clarion* reported on July 21 that a KKK meeting drew about 2000 participants in Roseburg. The meeting was conducted on the town's outskirts while two crosses burned on hillsides nearby. After the reading of the Klan charter the participants held a big picnic.

The weekly *Medford Clarion* and its editor William Phipps supported the Klan and discredited Medford's elected officials as "the gang." Llewellyn Banks would later use that term in his newspaper, the *Medford Daily News*. The *Ashland Tidings* published positive articles about Klan activities and ran a quarter-page ad announcing, "Hear the Truth about the Ku Klux Klan by Dr. R.H. Sawyer, famous international lecturer."

In Jackson County, Klan influence could be seen in an attempt to recall Jackson County Sheriff Terrill. His intended successor was D.M. Lowe who was backed by the KKK. Lowe also promised that he would enforce prohibition laws from a higher moral ground then Sheriff Terrill had done. The *Mail Tribune* characterized the recall as, "Politics, politics, politics—secret society and personal —the desire of the "outs" to get in —there is the whole depressing business in a nutshell." Candidate and challenger D.M. Lowe proclaimed in the waning hours of the bitter recall campaign that he was not a KKK member. The final vote of the recall, July 31, 1922, was Terrill 2943, Lowe 2638. The *Mail Tribune* commented, "A great many people are wise after the event. What Oregon needs are more people wise before the event."

In early August 1922, the Medford grand jury heard 25 witnesses describe the attacks by the hooded vigilantes back in March. They told of men in hoods and gowns firing weapons, throwing a rope over a tree limb, and placing a noose around the victim's necks. The victims were lifted off the ground by the ropes, lowered, and then ordered out of the state. The grand jury indicted many men for these outrageous acts. In late August the defendants' lawyers challenged every charge. The case didn't reach trial until March 1923. Then the states assistant attorney general L.A. Liljeqvist was unable to convict the men. The defense attorneys discredited the victims so badly that the case was ultimately dismissed. The trial closely mirrored earlier cases where mobs had chased socialist Wobblies from Oregon towns. Juries refused to convict the lawless mobs, so they escaped all penalties.

The *Medford Clarion* claimed in an October 1922 issue that the *Mail Tribune* was "publishing sinister propaganda each day against the" KKK. *Clarion* editor Phipps railed against the Medford city council for prohibiting "members of this order (KKK) from wearing their regalia in any street, alley, or public place in the city." He emphasized the Klan values of prohibition and Americanism.

Meanwhile, Ruhl continued his arguments against the Klan. He wrote that Oregon had seen unusual peace and prosperity before the Klan arrived. "Catholic worked with Protestant, Protestant with Catholic," but since the Klan had introduced the Compulsory Education Bill, intolerance was spreading. When Hall narrowly lost the Republican primary the Klan placed their hopes on Democratic governor aspirant Walter M. Pierce. Pierce accepted the Compulsory Education Bill as part of his election campaign.

Ruhl continued to support Governor Ben Olcott. But local Jackson county races were leaning against the "Independent American Voters League" a group of county voters opposed to the Klan.

The two largest issues in the 1922 general election were the governor's race and the initiative against parochial schools. On November 7, 1922 the voters made their decisions. Democrat Walter Pierce took the governor's race handily by 133,392 votes to Olcott's 99, 164. In Jackson County the vote was Pierce 4,670 to Olcott's 3,331. The Compulsory Education Bill was the real surprise of the election. The bill won statewide by 115,506 to 103,685, but in Jackson County the bill lost 3637 to 3262. Robert Ruhl was more than a little discouraged. Not only did his candidate lose but also the Compulsory Education initiative won.

Ruhl had had enough of politics for a while. "Forget it," he wrote. Oregon needs "a strong pull together." He also noted "the Compulsory School Bill allows a four year's breathing space, before it becomes effective." The new law would not take effect until 1926. But in 1924 the Oregon district court ruled it unconstitutional. Governor Pierce appealed the decision to the U.S. Supreme Court, which unanimously upheld the lower court's decision in 1925. The, anti-Catholic bill backed by the Ku Klux Klan died in the courts before it became law.

Ruhl's attempt to convince the states electors to vote against the Compulsory Education Bill failed; Governor Olcott sent Ruhl a personal letter thanking him for his editorial efforts. "It is a pleasure for me to once more thank you for your splendid friendship and support. I have no great personal regret over the result. The desire for change seemed nationwide. In leaving the office I am happy to do so with a clear conscience and the feeling that the principles my friends and I stood for are immutably right and eventually must prevail."

Governor Ben Olcott
Photo from the Oregon State Library in Salem

Ruhl's gutsy stand against the KKK cost him some subcribers, but it also won him respect, notably from the Catholic community, and from a number of Oregon newspapers. The *Pendleton Tribune* for example, asked for professional help in handling KKK issues in northeast Oregon. After the election battles of 1922 the KKK's invisible empire slowly lost credibility. But, the *Medford Mail Tribune* had gained a reputation as a fighter for law, order and sanity.

Ruhl's independent attitude would guide him and the *Tribune* through the twenties. During that era, Ruhl's beloved Jackson County and its agricultural industry prospered. Ruhl was in his late 40s and had a successful newspaper business, with 5000 subscriptions. He and his wife Mabel had two daughters.

Still, as tranquil as everything seemed to be, dark clouds were gathering. First came the thunder of the Great Depression—"Black Tuesday" on October 29,1929. Ever optimistic, the *Mail Tribune* wrote, "The Wall Street collapse had scarcely started before the President (Herbert Hoover) got busy. In short he is the real leader when leadership is the supreme need." Unfortunately, the President's efforts wouldn't help Medford much.

Mabel Ruhl, c1930
Photo from Southern Oregon Historical Society collection

Ruhl's fight against the Ku Klux Klan had prepared him for dealing with government weirdos, but had it prepared him enough? In the early 1930s Ruhl and the *Medford Mail Tribune* would have to face another political upheaval. The economic turmoil sparked political unrest in Jackson County as it did all over the country. In 1929 a shrewd, articulate leader emerged to rouse the discontented. Llewellyn A. Banks bought the *Medford Daily News* and soon became a firebrand for rebellion. Along with Earl H. Fehl, editor and publisher of the *Pacific Record Herald*, he savagely attacked Medford's leaders and the editor of the *Mail Tribune*, Robert Ruhl. Ruhl had his hands full, fending off these attacks while trying to keep the *Mail Tribune* financially solvent.

The Trial –
May 8 through May 12, 1933

May 8, 1933

When the trial had adjourned at noon on Saturday the 6th Mr. and Mrs. Banks were escorted to the Lane County jail to eat lunch. While they were eating reporters were allowed in, to ask questions. *Ashland Tidings* reporter G.M. Green asked Banks if he was going to testify. "I want to testify. I hope I can take the stand. It is not for me to say. It is a matter for my lawyers to decide, of course. But I have a story to tell." Banks was asked his reflections on the trial. "We have nothing to say in criticism of the trial, so far. Judge

Inside the Lane County Jail
Photo from the Lane County Historical Society collection

Skipworth is pre-eminently fair. We have no worries." Later Banks showed a reporter his cell, and in one corner of it was a large bowl of spring blossoms. Other then the flowers the cell was a dark and dreary place.

While spring burst forth outside another week of trial for the Banks began. On Monday when the Banks' entered the courtroom it was packed with spectators. Mr. and Mrs. Banks sat behind their battery of lawyers, and behind the Banks were Mr. and Mrs. Charles P. Moran of Cleveland. One reporter observed, "Mr. Moran is a man of about 60 years—a typical successful Midwest business man, of evident wealth and refinement. His wife, Llewellyn's sister, is a woman about 50 years old. She dresses in excellent taste, and is ever a highly interested listener to the testimony. She consoles Mrs. Banks from time to time. Moran retained attorneys Lonergan and Hardy for the defense." People wondered if Mr. Banks would exhibit the same composure as he did the past week—smiling when things were going his way and rocking nervously in his chair when witnesses spoke harshly of him. One reporter noted that Banks seemed to have lost some weight.

Mr. C.A. Warren, having already been sworn in, was recalled for further examination.

On cross-examination by Lonergan, Mr. Williams testified about his position in the back yard and how he came to enter the house from the front porch.

Q. And at that time when you entered the Banks home who all were present?

A. Sergeant Lumsden, Sergeant O'Brien, and Mrs. Banks.

Q. And you found Mrs. Banks where?

A. She was sitting in the living room.

Q. Now, you immediately proceeded then to question Mrs. Banks, did you?

A. Shortly after getting in there, yes sir.

Q. Well now, you had Mrs. Banks go over this statement on three different occasions, as I understand it?

A. Not all the way through, no. The first time we only, you might say, started and the second time we were interrupted when the daughter came in.

Q. Yes, and it was only after her third recital that she spoke about "we" having shot Prescott, that's true, is it not?

A. That's correct, yes sir.

Q. She made no such statement to you the first or second time that she was telling the story?

A. No sir, I had asked her as to who had fired the shot and she said Mr. Banks had and the third time when she was at the door she told of opening the door and passing out the letters and she said Mr. Prescott tried to come in and "we had to shoot him."

At this point Lonergan tried to confuse the witness as to how many shots had been fired and how many people were in the house. Lonergan also tested how well he remembered the number of times he went to the house after the murder. But Williams would not fall for any of it. He stayed his ground. Lonergan changed course.

Q. When you visited the Banks home did you pick up something and take it away with you?

A. The only other article I took from the house was the letter that is referred to last Saturday, which was found in his coat pocket in Mr. Banks bedroom.

Q. When did you take that?

A. I do not recall that time but I did mark the letter and marked the date on the letter.

Q. You don't know which one of your searching visits there to the house that you got that letter?

A. I don't recall definitely, no, sir.

This exchange was followed by other attempts to discredit the officer in front of the jury. The exchange would lead to one of the most interesting developments of the trial.

Mr. Lonergan: I think that is all.

The Court: Is that all, Mr. Moody?

Mr. Moody: Just a moment, if the Court please, I will get State's Exhibit A-11 for identification.

REDIRECT-EXAMINATION by Mr. Moody:

Q. I hand you State's Exhibit A-11 for identification and ask you if that is the letter that you found in the coat pocket that counsel on cross-examination was inquiring about?

A. It is, yes, sir.

Mr. Moody: *I offer the same in evidence, State's Exhibit A-11.*

The Court: *Exhibit A-11. Submit it to counsel.*

(State's Exhibit A-11 is handed to counsel for the defendants.)

Register-Guard reporter Marian Lowry called it the most "suspenseful" moment in the trial. The letter was referred to as the "To Daddy from Mother." Everyone in the courtroom was tense and straining to see the sheet of paper as it was handed to the defense team. They all huddled around the table reading the document with the Banks' and Moran's looking over the defense lawyer's shoulders.

Mr. Lonergan: *If the Court pleases, on behalf of the defendants and each of them, we desire to interpose an objection to the offer of 17-11—*

The Court: *A-11.*

Mr. Lonergan: *A-11 for identification on the ground that it is incompetent, irrelevant and immaterial and not within any of the issues of the case.*

The Court: I don't see how you claim that letter to be competent. There is not any identification as to who wrote the letter.

Mr. Moody: Well, if the Court pleases, I wish to refresh you Honor's mind. On the cross-examination of---

The Court: It is an extremely prejudicial letter. It isn't identified. There isn't any testimony as to who wrote the letter. Anyone of a thousand people might write a letter to Mr. Banks and yet it would not be binding on him.

Mr. Moody: ....I think that I have connected it. I think the state has connected it, and that counsel's examination has connected it....

After a somewhat lengthy rebuttal in which the state tried again to admit the letter, the Court saw it differently and cited State vs. Laundy, in a lengthier redress, ending:

The Court: ...Now there isn't any evidence whatsoever as to who wrote the letter. Not a scintilla of testimony. A thousand people may have written a letter to the defendant Banks, and yet unless there was some act on his part to make it competent it would not at all be binding upon him, and I think it is an error to admit this letter.... at this time it isn't competent. (The defense attorney's objection was sustained.)

Even though the contents of the letter were not revealed to the jury, the prosecution thought it might further strengthen their case against Mrs. Banks. But for now, the letter was ruled out.

Continuing testimony of Sergeant Warren confirmed that his search of the Banks' bedroom had turned up a suitcase that contained ammunition, a pistol and rifle, two woolen shirts, boots, and soap. Next to the bag was a hunting coat and hat. The prosecution maintained that it showed that Banks had intended to leave town after the killing. The defense countered that Banks had been merely getting ready for a hunting trip to get away from the strain he was under.

The next prosecution witness was Clatous McCredie. After being first duly sworn to tell the truth, the whole truth and nothing but the truth, he was questioned by Moody.

Q. State you name?

A. Clatous McCredie.

Q. Where do you reside?

A. Medford, Oregon.

Q. What is you official position?

A. Chief of Police for six years.

Q. Were you in the city of Medford on the 16th day of March, 1933?

A. I was.

Q. Did you go up to the residence of Mr. and Mrs. Banks, that day?

A. I did.

Q. What time did you go?

A. About ten-thirty.

Q. What was your business there?

A. Captain Bown came into my office and told me---

Q. Don't talk so fast.

A. Captain Bown came into my office and told me what had happened. Lieutenant Dunn and myself went up there immediately and went out West Main Street to the Banks' residence.

Q. Speak a little louder.

A. And as we approached the Banks residence, we noticed Sergeant Warren and Lumsden out near the Banks' garage. We drove west past the Banks' house then into Quince Street, stopped the car, got out, and stood on the sidewalk.

Q. Who?

A. Lieutenant Dunn and I, and Jimmy O'Brien—we drove just past

76

Jimmy before we stopped the car and then he came up and talked to us, stood there and talked just a few minutes wondering what to do and then I went over to a house across the street and called my office. There was nobody in and then I tried to call a couple of the boys on the telephone and couldn't get hold of them.

Q. Go ahead.

A. Then I went back outside and met Lieutenant Dunn and Sergeant O'Brien again. That was about a hundred feet west of the Banks residence. We were standing there talking and the crowd began to gather, when Gordon Kershaw brought a note up, accompanied by Tommy Williams.

Q. Go ahead.

A. And we read the note and then we started over towards the house. Sergeant Dunn was the first man on the porch.

Q. I hand you State's Exhibit A-9 (note on blotter) and ask you if you recognize that?

A. Yes, Sir.

Q. Well, then, what did you do?

A. I went over to the porch and Lieutenant Dunn walked up on the porch and came back down and I walked up and looked at Mr. Prescott.

Q. Was he dead at that time?

A. He was dead, yes, sir, and I stayed there for a considerable time, then the first thing we knew about anything going on, why, deputy Sheriff Lowd and Captain Bown came up and they were let in the house. I stayed on the porch then until they started to come out and I walked out to the car and opened the door.

Q. Did they come out alone?

A. Came out with Mr. Banks, one on each side of him, and I walked ahead of him and made the crowd stand back and opened the door to the Nash sedan and let them in and shut the door, and they left and we went back on the porch and stood there until the coroner took Mr. Prescott away.

Q. Did you go in the house then?

A. After Mr. Prescott was taken away I went into the house.

Q. Who was in there then?

A. Sergeants O'Brien, Lumsden, Warren and Vern Shangle and the sheriff.

Q. Was Mrs. Banks there?

A. She was not.

Q. Who took her away?

A. I saw them leaving outside the house. I don't know who took her.

Mr. Moody: *You may cross-examine.*

Mr. Longeran: *You have been the chief of Police of the City of Medford for six years?*

A. The 15th of January, yes sir.

Q. You were not a member of the Good Government Congress that was formed down there in Jackson County, were you?

A. No, sir.

Q. And Mr. Wilson, the Mayor of the city, didn't belong to that either?

A. Not to my knowledge, no sir.

Q. Did you attend any of the meetings of that Good Government Congress?

A. No, sir.

Q. Never did?

A. No, sir.

Q. They had a number of meetings down there in and about Medford?

A. Yes, sir.

Then came the testimony of Miss Charlotte Deford under direct-examination by Mr. Moody.

Mr. Moody: *Now, speak loud and clear. Where do you reside?*

A. Tillamook.

Q. Are you related to Lieutenant Dunn in the police service?

A. He is my brother-in-law.

Q. Were you in Medford on March 16, 1933?

A. Yes, sir.

Q. What caused you to go the Banks' home?

A. I was over at Mrs. Ellenburg's and the Lieutenant called up on the telephone and asked me to come over and act as matron.

Q. And when you got there who was in the house?

A. Lieutenant Dunn, Mr. Lumsden, Mr. Warren and I think that was all just at that time, though Mr. O'Brien was in later and the photographers were in and the little girl was there part of the time.

Q. What did Mr. Dunn instruct you to do?

A. He instructed me to search Mrs. Banks. We went into the bedroom and I searched her.

Q. While you were there did you have any conversation with Mrs. Banks?

A. Well, very little. I know when I searched her I said I was sorry I had to search her, and then at one time when she was getting ready to leave, when she was powdering and putting on her hat, she said that Mr. Banks had been terribly persecuted since he had been in Medford, and then the little girl said, "Why did he have to kill somebody?" and that's all the conversation, I think, just about.

Q. Did you hear her have any conversation with Mr. Warren and Mr. Lumsden?

A. Yes, she went through the story twice in my presence.

Q. After that what happened?

A. Well, after that then we went down to the police station. The little girl—well, I didn't tell about when the little girl came in. You didn't ask me.

Q. Tell about that.

A. Between the two stories that she told me, when we were sitting in chairs, Mrs. Banks with her back to the French doors and Mr. Warren and myself—

Q. Speak up louder.

A. Why, Mr. Warren had just asked her a question and he was writing it down when a little girl burst into the room and was crying and she said, "Oh, Mother, what's the matter?" And Mrs. Banks said, "Your father shot Mr. Prescott." And the little girl said, "Oh, Mother, I knew he would do it." No, she said first, the little girl said, "Oh, Mother, is he dead?" Mrs. Banks said, "I don't know," says, "He is lying out there on the porch or he was." Then the little girl said—

Mr. Lonergan: *I want to interpose an objection and ask that that be stricken from the record.*

The Court: *Yes, the conversation what the little girl said is stricken out. The jury will disregard it.*

CROSS-EXAMINATION by Mr. Lonergan:

Q. Is it Miss or Mrs.?

A. Miss.

Q. Were you ever called in before to do any matron work?

A. No, sir.

Q. That was the first time that you ever had been asked to assist in any police work of any kind?

A. Yes, sir.

Q. How long did you remain there in the room with Mrs. Banks and the others whom you have named before conducting her to the bedroom for investigation or examination?

A. Why, it couldn't have been but just a moment or two because the Lieutenant then took me right up to Mrs. Banks and said this ---he said, "You have been placed under arrest and this is – this lady will act as matron and search you," and Mrs. Banks immediately stood up, and I didn't know whether to search her there or where, and they said, "You can go to the bedroom," and we went right into the bedroom and I searched her and we came out almost immediately.

Q. And so you were instructed then in the presence of Mrs. Banks that you were to search her and watch out for her?

A. Well, stay with her.

Q. Were you armed?

A. No, sir.

Q. You have talked this over considerably of course?

A. Of course all my bridge clubs have to know about it and all those things.

Q. What?

A. You have to tell it to your bridge club and such things as that.

(The last answer caused a ripple of laughter from the spectators)

The Court: *Have order in the courtroom.*

Q. Let's get down to the door. Isn't it a fact when Mrs. Banks called attention of the officers to the door and said, "See what he did to the door," that she showed them where the strip on the side of the door jam had been pulled apart?

A. She didn't designate anything there. She says, "See, just about like that, see what he did to the door." And that was all.

Q. Did the officers then examine the door?

A. Not before me.

Q. So after the statement was made by Mrs. Banks, "See what he did to the door." —by "he" she was talking about Mr. Prescott, I believe you said?

A. Yes, sir.

Q. You left with Mrs. Banks, didn't you?

A. Yes, sir.

Q. And took her down to the jail?

A. Yes, sir.

Q. And how long did you stay there with her?

A. It was probably a little over an hour. I think it must have been somewhere near eleven o'clock when I first went to the house, and then shortly after we got to the police station they asked me to look after the little girl until someone came for her, and I remember the twelve o'clock whistle blowing, and then I stayed with the little girl until one-fifteen.

Q. And then your relations as matron there were ended?

A. Yes, sir.

Mr. Lonergan: *That is all, your Honor.*

The next witness that was questioned was Sergeant A. K. Lumsden. Other than spectators getting another chuckle out of the handling of the unloaded rifle by the witness, who innocently pointed it at the judge, Lumsden's testimony under direct-examination and cross-examination corroborated testimony already given earlier in the trial. Next up was prosecution witness Phil Lowd. He was sworn in to tell the truth, the whole truth and nothing but the truth.

DIRECT-EXAMINATION BY Mr. Moody:

Q. State you name.

A. Phillip Lowd.

Q. Speak up loud. The acoustics in this room aren't very good. Where do you live?

A. Medford.

Q. What is your business?

A. I am connected with the sheriff's office.

Q. In what capacity?

A. Deputy sheriff.

Q. Were you in Medford on March 16, 1933?

A. Yes, sir.

Q. And did you go to the residence of Mr. and Mrs. Banks?

A. Yes, sir.

Q. At what time?

A. At about five minutes to eleven.

Q. What was the purpose of your visit?

A. About twenty minutes to eleven I received a telephone call from the sheriff's office telling me to go directly to the police office as soon as possible. Captain Bown of the state police met me. We got into his car and went directly to the Banks' home.

Q. As you went in the front door did you see anything on the front porch?

A. I saw Mr. Prescott's body lying on the right side of the door.

Q. Dead or alive?

A. Dead.

Llewellyn Banks' home
Photo from the Southern Oregon Historical Society collection

Q. Did you see anything else on the porch?

A. I saw two letters lying on the mat in front of the door.

(Counsel obtains the exhibits)

The Court: *They are marked A-18 (envelope), A-19 (letter), A-20 (envelope), and A-21 (letter). The letter was in duplicate and had been typed by Mrs. Banks and read as follows: "I have committed no crime. I refuse to submit to arrest on charges framed by the power interests and Medford's old gang. Any effort to arrest me will result in bloodshed and probably my own death."*

Mr. Moody: *I hand you State's Exhibits and ask you if you ever saw them before?*

A. Yes, sir, I have.

Q. Are those the letters you found there?

A. Yes, sir.

Q. What did you do then?

A. I helped Herbert Brown move a cot from the ambulance up on the porch, up to the side of Mr. Prescott's body. About that time Captain Bown came up on the porch and I called his attention to these two letters lying on the mat. He picked them up and Mrs. Banks opened the door and Mr. Bown entered and I followed him.

Q. What did Mrs. Banks say to you?

A. As I first entered the door, I glanced through the room and noticed Mr. Banks standing in the dining room. Mrs. Banks was standing to the left of the door and the first thing that was said, Mrs. Banks said, "My God, I am glad it wasn't you."

The Court: *Was that in the presence of Mr. Banks?*

A. Yes, sir.

Mr. Moody: *Then what did you do?*

A. Mr. Banks had his hat and overcoat on with both hands in his pockets and he advanced to meet Captain Bown and they met in the center of the living room. He said, "Is this Captain Bown?" and he said "It is." And they shook hands, and he turned to me and says, "Hello Phil." We shook hands.

Q. Yes?

A. Lee asked him what he had in his pockets, "A gun"? He said, "No, if I did, I might be tempted to use it." Lee was on his left and I was on his right. We each had hold of his arms and proceeded out the front door to a car. We got into the car and proceeded north to Grants Pass.

Q. Did you have any conversation with Mr. Banks on the way?

A. Yes, sir.

Q. Who was in the car with you?

A. Captain Bown, myself, Mr. Banks, and Officer Pewter.

Q. What was that officer doing there?

A. He was driving the car.

Q. How did you sit in the car?

A. I was sitting on the right hand side, Mr. Banks in the center and Captain on the left, in the rear seat.

Q. When did the conversation from any of these parties first begin?

A. Oh, about the time we got out to the city limits of Medford. I think the first conversation that we had was, I asked Mr. Banks if he only fired one shot, or if there was more than one shot fired. He said, "No, I only fired one shot." I then asked him if he used the .44 six-shooter or the big gun, and he said, no, he used the 30-30. I then asked him if it was not the 30-06 Newton instead of the 30-30, and he said, "Yes". He reached into his pocket and took out six 30-06 cartridges and gave them to us. Captain Bown put these cartridges in his pocket.

The Court: *A-22 for identification (cartridges)*

Mr. Lonergan: *We object---*

The Court: *The objection is overruled. (The envelope containing six shells marked State's Exhibit A-22, is admitted in evidence.)*

Q. Was the conversation that Mr. Banks had with you officers voluntary and free?

A. Yes, sir.

Q. And not rendered under any duress or compulsion?

A. They were not.

Q. What else did he say?

A. He said that Mr. Prescott came to the door. Mrs. Banks answered the door and the chain was fastened on the inside, letting the door open possibly four inches and that she handed Mr. Prescott two letters that he had prepared for her, and if George had taken those letters and gone away, none of this trouble would have happened. He said, "George was an old timer, and that is the way with those fellows, they didn't know when to leave well enough alone." He said, "He tried to force his way into the house and I shot him the same as I would any other burglar."

Q. Did Mr. Bown have any conversation with him in your presence?

A. Why, Mr. Bown asked him about these letters and he said one of them was addressed to him and one to Chief of Police McCredie, and Mr. Bown asked him if it would be permissible to open that letter and he said, "Yes, I wish you would for it is very important." And while going down the road after this conversation about the letters Captain opened the letter addressed to him and read it.

Mr. Moody: *The State now offers in evidence State's Exhibit A-20 (envelope) and A-21 (letter).*

Mr. Lonergan: *We desire, if you Honor please, to object....*

The Court: *The objection will be overruled.*

(Mr. Moody reads to the jury state's Exhibit A-21:) *"March 13, 1933, Chief of Police McCredie, Captain Lee Bown, Gentlemen: I have committed no crime and I will therefore refuse to submit to arrest on charges framed by the power interests and Medford's old gang. Any effort to arrest me will result in bloodshed and no doubt my death. I am willing to furnish bonds signed by Mrs. Banks and myself, which is backed by half a million dollars worth of property in Jackson County and will appear in a court of justice in answer to any charge which may be preferred against me. Very truly yours, Llewellyn A. Banks."*

Q. I will ask you if you had ever seen the rifle before to which he had referred?

A. Yes, sir.

Q. I hand you state's Exhibit A-4 and ask you whether or not that is the rifle?

A. Yes, sir.

Q. Had you ever seen the pistol before?

A. I have.

Q. I hand you State's Exhibit A-5 and ask you if that is the pistol....

A. It is.

Mr. Moody: *You may inquire.*

Mr. Lonergan: *Now, prior to the 16th day of March of this year as a deputy sheriff of Jackson County you had occasion to serve papers on Mr. Banks on numerous occasions, had you not?*

A. Yes, sir.

Q. About how many times would you say you had served Mr. Banks with papers?

A. I think about twenty-two or three different services.

Q. He had been sued down there on twenty-two or three different occasions by plaintiffs, had he not?

A. Yes, sir.

Q. And the papers were placed in the hands of the sheriff and you served them? Is that right?

A. I did.

The cross-examination by Lonergan went over much of the testimony already covered by the prosecution. Lonergan attempted, without success, to confuse Lowd on his previous testimony. Next up for questioning was prosecution witness Rodney Roach.

Mr. Moody: *Where do you reside?*

A. Medford, Oregon.

Q. And what is you occupation?

A. State Police Officer in the Game Division.

Q. How long have you been such officer?

A. Since August 1st, 1931.

Q. Have you ever been in Llewellyn Banks' home?

A. I have.

Q. When?

A. March 16th.

Q. At what time?

A. At four o'clock in the afternoon.

Q. Were you alone?

A. Officer Walker went with me. Other people present in the house at that time Charlie Clause, Harry Ingling, Pete Martin, and Vern Carey.

Q. Did you make any search of the dwelling at that time?

A. We did, yes.

Q. And what did you find?

A. Officer Walker found in the hallway leading from the front part of the house, or from the dining room to the rear, on a cot a .32 automatic pistol.

Q. Was there just the pistol?

A. Holster, extra magazine and cartridges.

Q. Were you present when he found it?

A. I was, yes.

Q. Anything over it?

A. A lady's coat was laid over the pistol and holster and belt.

The Court: *What time of day was it?*

A. It was four twenty-five.

Mr. Moody: *(Handing witness Exhibit) Now be careful about this.*

This is loaded. (Handing witness State's Exhibit A-23 for identification)

The Court: *Let Mr. Roach handle it.*

Mr. Moody: *Be careful. It is loaded. Look out now for those shells.*

The Court: *Put the shells in an envelope.*

Mr. Moody: *The State offers in evidence State's Exhibit A-23 for identification, being a pistol, and State's Exhibit A-24, being bullets or cartridges which have just in open Court been extracted from said pistol.*

Mr. Lonergan: *This offer, Your Honor, is objected to, and my objections applies to both exhibits, 23 and 24, on the ground they are wholly incompetent, irrelevant and immaterial and not within any of the issues of this case and not within any of the material allegations of the indictment and not binding upon the defendant, or either of them. They were found long after the defendants had been taken from the house and as the evidence discloses here there were many and various people coming and going out of the house, and there is no connection in any way at all with these defendants, and that the offer is made for purposes of prejudice and that only.*

Mr. Moody: *It is not made for prejudice.*

The Court: *He is assigning his reason. Now the rifle and the forty-four were introduced in evidence because they were found in the house at the time of the alleged commission of the alleged crime. Now you are offering in evidence a revolver and shells, which the witness says was found in the residence of the defendant Banks several hours after the alleged commission of the alleged crime. It seems to me, at least it is a doubtful question, unless there is some showing that that revolver belongs to the defendant Banks or to the defendant Edith Banks, I doubt its competency. It may be. If you have any authority on that question I will be glad to hear it in the morning.*

Mr. Moody: *Did you find anything else in that residence?*

A. I did.

Q. What else?

A. In the fireplace I found one empty 30-06 cartridge. I kept it in my possession until I returned to the State Police office, and then I turned it over to Captain Bown.

The Court: *Let it be marked A-27.*

Mr. Moody: *I will ask you whether or not that that is the size of a cartridge that the rifle marked as State's Exhibit A-4 fits and uses?*

A. It is, yes.

Q. And who was with you when you found it?

A. Officer Walker, Charlie Clause.

Mr. Lonergan: We make the same objection,

The Court: *I will reserve ruling on that until morning.*

After defense cross-examination of Rodney Roach Monday afternoon it was five o'clock so Judge Skipworth ordered the jury to retire until the next morning at 9:30 o'clock. At that time cross-examination would continue. But after the jury had left they were recalled to the jury box.

The Court: *Mrs. Ludford, the bailiff, Mrs. Bailey, reports that you are ill and unable to continue upon this case.*

The Juror, Mrs. Ludford: *I would like to be excused.*

The Court: *I say are you able to proceed.*

The Juror: *I feel I can't go through. I have got more of a cold and feel I am not able to do it.*

The Court: *Let the record show that the juror, Mrs. Ludford, reports she is ill and unable to continue to serve as a juror in this case and she will therefore be dismissed and the Court will proceed to draw one of the alternates to serve as a juror. The alternates are R. Dunning, and Lee Young. Put their names in* *a box and shake it up and draw one of these alternate jurors to serve.*

The Clerk: *R. Dunning.*

The Court: *You are excused, Mrs. Ludford, and Mr. Dunning (an Oakridge laborer), you will take her place as a juror, and you will continue as an alternate, Mr. Young. The jury will take a recess until tomorrow morning at nine-thirty.*

(This ended the seventh day of the trial, the jury now composed of 7 men and 5 women. Of course the admissibility of the loaded revolver and additional ammunition found on the cot was very important to the prosecution's case. It showed premeditation and that Banks meant to back up his threats with bloodshed if warrants were given for his arrest. As one newspaper had reported Banks had an arsenal of loaded weapons at his disposal. In the living room he had the loaded rifle, a loaded .44 caliber revolver, and in the hallway another loaded revolver. The decision by Judge Skipworth would be pivotal.)

May 9, 1933

As the trial resumed Tuesday on a typical cloudy, rain-threatening day, the courtroom was packed again. The jury was now reduced to thirteen including one alternate. When they filed into the jury box one woman was wearing a white summer hat. Among the spectators, younger attorneys crowded into front row seats drawn, no doubt, by the trial's famous lawyers and the case's notoriety.

The evidence mentioned the previous day was about to be decided upon as to its admissibility. The jury was dismissed. Shortly afterwards the prosecution and the defense began their arguments. The exhibits in question were A-23 (pistol); A-24 (shells); A-25- (belt and holster); A-26 (shells); A-27 (empty 30-06 cartridge). These items had been found on the cot in the hallway. This part of the proceedings was not transcribed because the jury was not present. But newspaper articles called it a fiery session, a "bitter legal battle," becoming personal at times between Ralph Moody and Frank Lonergan.

Ralph Moody contended that the revolver showed, "The existence of a conspiracy, backed by a deliberate and premeditated plan in which both defendants took part. — and it was found where you would least expect to find it—hidden beneath a woman's coat. As such I have a duty alike toward the state and these defendants. If there was the slightest doubt as to the admissibility of these exhibits I would be the last to ask it, or want it."

Whereupon defense counsel Lonergan said, "There is no showing that the defendants owned or had anything to do with this revolver. The rifle has been introduced as the weapon used in the commission of the crime. A group running through the house found the revolver six hours after the commission of the crime. It is introduced here by the state in an effort to show that an arsenal existed in the Banks home. And to lead the jury into the realms of conjecture and speculation…the information presented here is done for prejudicial purposes and to inflame the minds of the jury."

When the arguments ended the Judge made his decision.

The Court: *The exhibits will be admitted in evidence, and the objections to the admission are overruled. The reasons for them being admitted as State's Exhibits: Under the charge of first degree murder the state must show intent, preparedness and premeditation. While it is admitted the weapon was not the one used in the alleged slaying of Prescott, it still has a bearing on the purported preparedness for battle of the defendants.*

Following the Judge's decision, the cross-examination by Mr. Lonergan of Rodney Roach resumed. The most interesting exchange happened when Roach was quizzed about a revolver he had identified, as a .32 the day before but now claimed was a .380.

Q. I suppose, Mr. Roach, that you have had considerable experience in the matter of firearms?

A. Some.

Q. Well, as an officer connected with the game department here for some nine years, I believe it was, you of course came across a great many varieties of guns, didn't you?

A. Yes, mostly rifles and shotguns.

Q. And you, of course, carried a revolver most of the time with you, yourself?

A. Yes.

Q. I am calling attention to State's Exhibit A-23, I believe that is the exhibit you say you found, or was found there on the cot in the hallway of the Banks' home. (Counsel handing exhibit to witness)

A. Yes.

Q. And that you say is a 32? A 32 automatic?

A. I think so.

The Court: See if the magazine is out?

A. Yes, it is out. No, it is a 380 instead of a 32.

Mr. Lonergan: What? (A witness to the trial said that at this point Lonergan leapt from his chair)

A. It is a 380 instead of a 32.

Q. It isn't a 32 at all, is it?

A. No.

Q. And these cartridges which you identified here yesterday as being 32 cartridges, would you say that that is what those cartridges are.

A. Those cartridges I said yesterday were the ones that were with the gun.

Q. Well, 32? You identified those cartridges as being 32 cartridges for the purpose of use in that gun, didn't you?

A. I don't think I said 32. I said they were cartridges for that gun.

Q. Well, you said the gun was a 32-caliber gun? Of course, the only cartridges that would fit it would be 32s?

A. If it was 32, yes.

Q. The fact is that is not a 32 automatic gun at all, is it?

A. No it is a 380.

The next prosecution witness was a uniformed Walter S. Walker affiliated with the state police residing in Klamath Falls. He corroborated most of what Mr. Roach had said, especially finding the murder weapon's spent cartridge in the ashes of the fireplace. State's exhibit A-27 was an empty 30-06 cartridge. On direct-examination Walker identified the shell. Not deterred in the slightest Lonergan attacked on his cross-examination.

Q. As far as the fireplace is concerned then all you know about it is that Roach called your attention to the fact that he had found a discharged shell there?

A. Yes, sir.

Q. A blank shell?

A. Yes, sir.

Q. And he didn't pick it up and hold it up for you to see, did he?

A. No, sir.

Q. But the ashes had all been scraped away so that you could see it lying there in the fireplace?

A. Yes, sir, I could see it.

Q. Then, it was picked up?

A. Yes, sir.

Q. By whom?

A. Officer Roach.

Q. And then you marked your initials on it, I believe?

A. Yes, sir.

The next prosecution witness was Keith K. Ambrose, Medford police officer. During the direct-examination it was learned that Ambrose had been on guard in the Banks home in the afternoon until 2:30 pm with Charles W. Clause, Ashland police officer. At one point in the cross-examination a testy Lonergan asked Ambrose if he wanted to argue.

Q. Who was guarding the front door while you two were back in the house?

A. If there had been anything at the front door we would have heard it.

Q. That isn't what I asked. I asked who was guarding the front door while you two were in the back bedroom?

A. There was no one inside as far as the inside of the house was concerned.

Q. In other words, you both wandered around through the house in the back bedrooms and nobody was at the front of the house watching the front door?

A. We never spent any considerable time in the other part of the house.

Q. But you won't answer the question. You want to argue. (One reporter said tempers flared.)

The Court: *Answer the question.*

Q. While you and Clause were going together into the back bedrooms, in the rooms at the north end of the house, which is the back end of the house, then there was no one at the front to watch the door?

A. Yes, sir.

The next witness for the prosecution was Charles William Clause, former chief of police of Ashland.

DIRECT-EXAMINATION by Mr. Moody:

Q. When were you Chief of Police at Ashland?

A. Up to the first of the year.

Q. Were you in Medford on March 16, 1933?

A. Yes, sir.

Q. Did you go to the Banks residence?

A. Yes, sir. It was approximately twelve-thirty when I was there.

Q. Did you meet anyone there?

A. Keith Ambrose.

Q. What did you do when you got there?

A. We watched the place. Kept the people out of it.

Q. How long did you remain there?

A. I remained there until two-thirty and then I left and went to lunch and came back.

Q. And who relieved you and Mr. Ambrose?

A. Mr. Pete Martin and Mr. Vern Carey.

Mr. Moody: *Take the witness.*

CROSS-EXAMINATION BY Mr. Lonergan:

Q. And what had you been doing since the first of the year?

A. Well, I practically haven't been doing anything.

Q. Well, Up to the 16th of March, from the first of the year up to and including the 16th day of March you were doing you say a little police work. What was the character of it?

A. Robbery.

Q. Who were you representing?

A. A man by the name of Perozie.

Q. That is, you were hired in the capacity of a private detective?

A. Yes, sir.

Q. How long did that last??

A. Well, I am still working on it.

Q. Oh, you haven't cleared that one up yet?

A. No, sir.

(One reporter said that Judge Skipworth had to rap his gavel for quiet because of the laughter.)

Q. And then you came to Medford?

A. Yes, sir. To the state police office.

Q. What was that for?

A. I went there to see if they needed anybody to help them.

Q. I see. You came up there to offer your service?

A. I certainly did.

Q. And the reason for that was that you didn't like Mr. Banks, wasn't it?

A. No, I didn't say I didn't like Mr. Banks.

Q. What?

A. No, I don't know that it was for that reason.

Q. Well, that was the reason now, wasn't it?

A. Well, I can't say particularly that it was.

Q. Well, whether it was particular or otherwise, that's the fact of the matter, isn't it?

A. For the simple reason I had been an officer so long and I wanted to help the boys out.

Q. You had been Chief of Police by appointment down there in

Ashland for four years?

A. Yes

Q. And you were not an officer after the first of January 1933?

A. No.

Q. And you came rushing up there to Medford as soon as you heard about this to get into it, didn't you?

A. I certainly did.

Q. And the reason that you did because you had an animosity towards Mr. Banks, that's correct isn't it?

A. I can't say that I did.

Q. Well, that fact of the matter is you did have an animosity towards him, didn't you?

A. Oh, to a certain extent I suppose.

Q. Well, yes, let's be honest about this thing now. He had written you up in the paper down there, hadn't he?

A. Well, in a certain way I suppose he had.

Q. But you do know as a matter of fact that you had a very strong animosity towards Mr. Banks?

A. To a certain extent, yes.

Q. Were you paid?

A. No, sir.

Q. So that your services out there as far as being sent to the Banks home was purely gratuitous on you part?

A. I never asked for any pay and never had any.

Mr. Lonergan: *And you were up there without any notion or hope of being paid by the state police?*

A. I never said anything about being paid.

Q. Were you in uniform when you went out there to the Banks residence?

A. I had on a suit something similar to this.

The Court: *Well now, he asked you if you were in uniform.*

Mr. Lonergan: *You know what uniform is?*

A. No, I was not in uniform.

Q. Was your appointment made in writing?

A. No sir, he just deputized me to go down there.

Q. How do you mean, just deputized you? Just told you to go?

A. Yes sir, Mr. Bown, Lee Bown.

Q. Just simply told you to go down there to the house?

A. Yes, sir.

Q. You took no oath of office?

A. No, sir.

Q. He didn't deliver or call you to take an oath to perform your duties at all?

A. No, sir.

Q. No, sir. Then when you went back there the second time on the 16th of March that you say was around three-thirty in the afternoon you stayed there until what time?

A. Five-thirty.

The cross-examination went on into the afternoon, and then the prosecution called Doctor C.I. Drummond a practicing physician and surgeon to the stand.

DIRECT-EXAMINATION by Mr. Moody:

Q. Where were you educated in your profession?

A. University of Nebraska, College of Medicine.

Q. And when did you graduate there?

A. January 1930.

Q. And are you a duly admitted and licensed practicing physician and surgeon in the state of Oregon and having a certificate therefore?

A. I do. I have.

Q. Do you occupy any particular official position in the county of Jackson in this state?

A. I am county health officer and coroner's physician.

Q. Did you hold an autopsy upon the body of one George Prescott? In March of this year?

A. I did.

Q. And what was the result?

A. The body had two major external wounds. One wound was on the left hand, the area about an inch and a half on the back of the left hand in the region of the knuckle of the index finger. The skin was gone and the last inch of the bone there was shattered, and around this wound were several superficial abrasions in which we found numerous pieces of splinters. The other wound was in the left side, about three inches below the tip of the shoulder on the front of the shoulder. That wound was about two inches in diameter. Under this superficial wound we found that the muscles under this here were badly torn and the fourth rib—about an inch and a half of the fourth rib was gone. Excuse me---a portion of the third rib was gone and the second and fourth ribs were shattered. On opening the chest we found that the left—the right pleural cavity was not abnormal. And the left chest cavity was filled with about a quart of blood, and this was removed and we found that the lung, both lobes of the lung, had an opening torn through them about probably an inch or an inch and a half in diameter. The sixth rib, right next to the spine, was shattered and on turning the body over we found a firm object in the same region, the sixth rib, just left of the spine. We made a small incision over this firm object and removed it. We gave the cause of death as "shock from an impact from some blunt object and internal hemorrhage."

Q. I hand you State's Exhibit A-10 and ask you if you recognize that.

A. Yes, I do.

Q. What is it?

A. It is identical with the object I removed from George Prescott.

CROSS-EXAMINATION by Mr. Lonergan:

Q. I believe, Doctor, as I recall it, you were assisted in that autopsy by Doctor B. C. Wilson?

A. I did the autopsy and doctor Wilson assisted me.

Q. All right. Now, this wound that was on the upper part of the chest on the left side, I believe you said?

A. Yes, sir.

Q. Was about two inches below the shoulder?

A. About three inches below the acromial process.

Q. Did you keep notes as you went along on the autopsy?

A. Yes, sir.

Q. Who kept the notes? Who took them down?

A. Mr. Looker.

Q. As you went along you described the results of the autopsy and what you found and it was taken down. Did Doctor Wilson take any notes?

A. They were taken down by Mr. Looker.

Q. Now, which way did this range as it entered in the upper part of the left chest? How did it range?

A. It ranged downward and back.

Q. Downward and back so that from the point of entrance to the place in the back where it had completed its course was about what distance?

A. I imagine about twelve inches, I couldn't say for sure because I didn't measure it.

Q. So that the statement thirteen inches would probably not be too much, would it?

A. No

Mr. Lonergan: *I think that is all, your Honor.*

(Witness excused)

The next prosecution witness to be sworn in was Gordon Kershaw.

DIRECT-EXAMINATION by Mr. Moody:

Q. Where do you live?

A. Medford, Oregon.

Q. What is your occupation?

A. Private citizen at the present time.

Q. Were you in Medford on the 16th of March 1933?

A. I was.

Q. I hand you State's Exhibit A-9 and ask you if you have ever seen that before? (It is a note written on a blotter by Mrs. Banks: "Come and get George Prescott and you will be all right. Then proceed in order.")

A. I have.

Q. Under what circumstances did you see it?

A. It was handed to me by Mr. Tommy Williams.

Q. All right. What did you do with it?

A. I kept it until I saw Mr. O'Brien and I gave it to him.

Q. Was there anybody with Jimmy O'Brien at the time that you gave it to him?

A. Yes, chief of police McCredie and several other people that were strangers to me.

Q. Is that note in the same condition now as it was at the time that you saw it?

A. It is.

Mr. Moody: *You may inquire.*

CROSS EXAMINAITON by Mr. Lonergan:

Q. You have examined the Exhibit A-9 that was handed to you?

A. I have.

Q. Then I direct your attention to the initials that appear in that upper left hand corner, were they there?

A. No sir.

Q. And the ones that appear down on the left hand side, and the ones on the extreme right hand corner, were those there?

A. No, sir.

Q. This is not identically in exactly the same—

A. It is the same note that was handed to me.

Q. I am asking you about this exhibit now. You are not trying to argue with me, I hope?

A. No, sir.

Q. So that this exhibit that has been introduced in evidence is not identically the same as it was when you handed it to O'Brien?

A. The same note I handed to O'Brien.

Q. Were the initials on it when you handed it to O'Brien?

A. No, sir.

Q. Then it is not the same?

A. Yes, sir.

Q. Well, all right.

(Noisy reaction from the courtroom)

The Court: I don't want any more demonstration in this courtroom.

Mr. Lonergan: That is all. (Witness excused)

Then came consultations between Judge Skipworth, Mr. Moody and Mr. Lonergan in which they all agreed to a recess from Tuesday afternoon until Thursday morning, the May 11th at 9:30am.

And so at 3:40 pm. in the afternoon of May 9th, the trial recessed. Earlier in the day, during breaks, Mr. Banks could be seen in conferences with his brother-in-law Charles Moran and his lawyers, Phipps and Enright. The next day there was much speculation about the case from reporters, spectators and participants. The *Medford Mail Tribune* quoted spectators asking, "How could this nice older couple ever be convicted of that horrible crime?" Some people were giving the Banks a 50-50 chance of acquittal. Reporters were less sure; as the prosecution's evidence mounted they stayed mum about the chances of Llewellyn Banks and his wife getting off.

Robert Ruhl wrote a letter with encouragement to Prosecutor Moody. Moody wrote back that he would be diligent and had great help from the state police, Jackson County's district attorney and many more people. Then he said, "I am conducting this case to the best of my ability, and shall continue to do so. I desire to be polite, but unmistakably firm, and to handle myself in the court in a lawyer-like manner, so as to entitle me to enjoy the respect and confidence of the judge and jury."

A spokesman for the defense stated, "We will show that Mr. and Mrs. Banks are not guilty on the indictment of first degree murder, and we will introduce several points of evidence to prove it. We will not make our stand on insanity alone, although Banks was not responsible for his actions at the time of the tragedy." Of course they didn't mention that Banks had tried to get them to blame the shooting on another man, who supposedly fled the house after the shooting. The defense even speculated that Banks might take the stand in his own defense.

Both the prosecution and defense used the recess day to pre-pare for Thursday the 11th. The prosecution had saved for last its most important witness, Lee Bown, acting captain of the southern district of the state police department. He had arrested Banks after the murder. Reporters also thought the prosecution would try once again to get the "Daddy Dear" letter admitted as evidence in the State's case. The letter would show that Mr. and Mrs. Banks were working together in the murder of Officer Prescott. Meanwhile the defense was marshaling witnesses, and was said to have thirteen lined up and ready to go, should the state rest its case early on Thursday.

While the lawyers were hard at work the jury residing in the

The Osburn Hotel dining room
Photo from the Lane County Historical Society collection

Osburn Hotel was living in relative luxury. At least that was the scene depicted when the jury came for its meals in the Osburn Hotel dinning room. The five women often talked gaily and wore colorful ensembles. One even wore flashy hats. The seven men were reported as being more solemn. Perhaps because they had to read newspapers that had been stripped of trial information, and were restricted from conversing with anyone accept fellow jury members and the bailiffs, they might have felt like they were as much in isolation as being in jail. While the jury ate at the Osborn, Mrs. Banks was allowed to join her husband for lunch at the Lane County jail. It was said that when she was there on the tenth she held a pink rose in her hand.

What was missing in all this was an acknowledgment of the murdered victim, George Prescott. The only remorse shown so far in the entire trial had been expressed by Ruth May, Mrs. Banks' young daughter. As a witness said she had been crying and asked her mother, "why did Daddy kill Prescott?" All other information during the trial appeared to be expressed factually. There was no doubt about who killed Officer Prescott: Llewellyn Banks had used

his 30.06 high-powered game rifle, leveled on his shoulder and at point-blank range. The soft-nosed bullet that ripped through his body had left a gaping two-inch hole. Up to this point in the trial the defense had deflected the emotional impact this trial should have represented—the merciless killing of a police officer. The defense was doing one hell of a job.

May 11, 1933

Mrs. Banks
Photo from the Southern Oregon Historical Society collection

On Thursday morning at 9:30am the trial commenced with another crowded courtroom. This would be the prosecutions last real opportunity to show the jury beyond all doubt that Mr. and Mrs. Banks conspired in the first-degree murder of Officer Prescott.

The Court: *Call your next witness.*

DIRECT-EXAMINATION by Mr. Moody:

Q. Give your full name.

A. Marjorie Saterlee.

Q. Where do you live?

A. Medford, Oregon—no, Roseburg, pardon me.

Q. When did you reside in Medford?

A. Up until March 1st of this year.

Q. Are you acquainted with Mr. and Mrs. Llewellyn A. Banks, the defendants in this case?

A. I am.

Q. How long have you known them?

A. About three years I should say.

Q. Were you employed by either of them?

A. Yes.

Q. In what capacity?

A. As secretary to Mr. Banks.

Q. And when?

A. On March—May 31st—no, pardon me, that's wrong. From May 30th, 1930, until February 26, 1931.

The Court: *1931?*

A. 1932.

Mr. Moody: *Q. Are you acquainted with the endearing terms that Mr. and Mrs. Banks referred to each other?*

A. Yes.

Q. And what were they?

A. She referred to Mr. Banks as "Daddy dear", and "Daddy". He referred to her as "Mother".

Q. Did you frequently hear them indulge in such expressions?

A. Yes.

Q. Do you know whether or not they ever indulged in such expressions in writing to each other?

A. Yes, frequently.

Q. Did you ever see Mrs. Banks Write?

A. yes.

Q. Are you familiar with her handwriting?

A. Yes.

Q. I hand you State's Exhibit A-11 for identification and ask you to examine it. From your examination of it can you state who wrote it?

A. Yes.

Q. Who?

Mr. Lonergan: Just a moment. We object. It doesn't tend to prove any of the material allegations of the indictment; There is no qualification on the part of the witness, and the witness has testified that she was in a secretarial capacity and under the provisions of the law, it is a confidential nature and is not permitted to be used in testimony without the consent of the employer.

The Court: *Have you laid a foundation? Did you ask her if she knew Mrs. Banks?*

Mr. Moody: *Yes, I asked her and she said she had frequently seen her write and knew her handwriting.*

The Court: Read the question.

(The reporter reads the last question, asking if she can say who wrote the note)

The Court: This is a preliminary question. She may answer that question.

A. Mrs. Banks.

Q. Mrs. Edith Banks? The defendant in this case?

A. Yes, sir.

Mr. Moody: Now, if the Court please, I offer it in evidence. (Counsel hands Exhibit A-11 to the Court)

The Court: There isn't any date on that.

Mr. Moody: No.

The Court: There isn't any particular person referred to in that note. I think it comes within the case of State vs. Myers. More in the nature of a threat.

Mr. Moody: If your Honor please, if you have some doubt I would like to be heard on it.

The Court: I don't believe, Mr. Moody, that that testimony is competent.

Mr. Moody: I would like to present this, if the Court wants to excuse the jury.

The counsel's argument was not transcribed because the jury was out of the room. But the Court's decision was written down.

The Court: Now, preliminarily to my ruling on the admissibility of this exhibit, I may state that the state of Oregon of course is entitled to present its theory of the case to the jury. The state of Oregon is entitled to make out its case, and it is the duty of the Court to admit all evidence offered by the state that is competent. However, here is a letter signed "Mother" and addressed to "Daddy dear". There is no date upon the letter. There is no evidence as to when it was admitted—was written. There is no evidence in the case as to who was meant in the letter "If you are going to fight that should be from home." That's in the letter. "If you are going to fight officers when they come to the house to serve a warrant on you," that would be an entirely different question and would probably render the letter competent in evidence. But here's a general letter. There is no specific class of persons indicated in the letter or anything in the letter. There is no indication as to who Banks intended to fight. There is no indication in the letter as to whom Mrs. Banks was advising him to fight. It certainly comes squarely within the case of State vs. Myers, and to my mind it would be glaring error to admit the letter and if there should be a conviction in this case it is my opinion that it would be reversible error and the Court will sustain the objection.

(The jury returned to the jury box)

The Court: *Any further use of this witness?*

Mr. Moody: *He said they wouldn't care to cross- examine so I will call another.*

The Court: *All right. Call another witness. (Witness excused)*

Edward H. Thomas was produced as a witness on the part of the State.

DIRECT-EXAMINATION by Mr. Moody:

Q. Where do you reside?

A. Medford, Oregon.

Q. What is your occupation?

A. Auditor for the State Industrial Accident Commission.

Q. What territory are you assigned to?

A. Jackson, Klamath and Lake Counties.

Q. And what are your duties?

A. My duties, to go around the different businesses under the State

Industrial Insurance Act, audit the books, and collect money.

Q. You're headquartered out of Medford?

A. Yes, sir.

Q. Do you know Mr. Llewellyn A. Banks, one of the defendants in this case?

A. I do.

Q. And have you met him?

A. I have.

Q. When?

A. Oh, I have known Mr. Banks for possibly two or three years. The last time I met Mr. Banks was on March 14th in the morning, after I called at his house to get hold of Black Channel mine, which Mrs. Banks—

The Court: *which Mr. Banks?*

A. Of which Mr. Banks was the president of the company and also the custodian of the records.

Mr. Moody: *And you called on him that day in the line of your duty in connection with the State Accident Commission?*

A. Yes, in his house. I called on him in the morning.

Q. Relate the conversation.

A. I went up to the house and rang the doorbell and Mr. Banks came to the door and invited me in. I told Mr. Banks that I wanted to get hold of the payroll of the Black Channel mine, as there had been an accident reported to the Commission, and there had been no fees collected, and that Salem was insisting on the payroll, and I had made several attempts to get the payroll but so far had not succeeded. I told Mr. Banks if I did not get the payroll that I would have to issue a subpoena. And when I told him that, he was sitting in the living room in his big easy chair, and I was sitting opposite from him, and when I said, "Issue a subpoena", he said, "Why, God damn you."

Mr. Lonergan: Your Honor, I am going to object to this.

Mr. Moody: If the Court please—

Mr. Lonergan: Just a minute. I would like to make my objection. I object to it as incompetent, irrelevant and immaterial and not within any of the issues of the indictment. Is here for prejudicial purposes, and is a matter that under the law of the Industrial Accident Commission is not a public matter, but is a matter between the Industrial Accident Commission and the employer, and is not a matter that is admissible in any court of record.

The Court: Of course I have no means of knowing what you intend to show by this witness. Of course it is often said that you can't un-ring the bell, so if the statement goes in evidence and isn't competent—

Mr. Moody: Well, your Honor to be perfectly fair with the Court, I will show what the witness will testify to. (Counsel handing paper to the Court)

The Court: Well, show it to counsel as well.

(The paper referred to is handed to counsel for the defendants.)

The Court: Of course so far as any statement or threats made concerning this witness—

Mr. Moody: I am not claiming it but it is all a part of the case.

The Court: I think the conversation is competent. I think the evidence is competent. I will overrule the objection.

Mr. Moody: Now, you start from where you used the curse word and proceed.

A. He said, "God damn you," he said, "I will pluck your heart out or any other man's heart out that comes up to this door to serve papers on me", and he was sitting in a chair near the fireplace, a little towards the east, and he stooped up and just as if picking up a rifle and said (witness indicating) "I can pluck any man's heart out that comes up to this door." I was dumbfounded for a minute.

The Court: *You needn't say that you were dumbfounded.*

Mr. Moody: *What door was he talking about?*

A. *The front door. And I said to Mr. Banks, "Surely you wouldn't be foolish enough to do anything like that?" and just at that time the doorbell rang and a man and lady went in and I went out.*

Mr. Moody: *You may inquire.*

CROSS-EXAMINATION by Mr. Lonergan:

Q. *You went into Mr. Banks' home there on the 14th of March on the business of the Industrial Accident Commission?*

A. *Yes, sir.*

Q. *You are not claiming to the jury that Mr. Banks had a rifle on the floor there?*

A. *No, sir.*

Q. *Why did you say he picked up a rifle? It may have been some other gun.*

A. *I said he made the motion as if he were.*

Q. *Picked up a rifle you said?*

A. *Yes, sir.*

Q. *Why did you say rifle?*

A. *Naturally when one points this way (indicating) he would have a rifle.*

Q. *Well, it might have been a shotgun, wouldn't it?*

A. *Yes, sir.*

Q. *Just why did you use the word "rifle" now here in this case?*

A. *That I couldn't say.*

Q. *You couldn't say that. I think that's all. (Witness excused)*

Lee Bown, produced as a witness on the part of the State testified next.

DIRECT-EXAMINATION by Mr. Moody:

Q. State you're name in full.

A. Lee M. Bown.

Q. Where do you reside?

A. Medford, Oregon.

Q. Do you occupy any official position in the state?

A. At the present time connected with the state police department and acting in the capacity of captain of Southern District No. 3.

Q. How long have you been connected with the police department?

A. Since August first, 1931.

Q. I will ask you if you were in the City of Medford, Oregon, Jackson County on the 16th day of March 1933?

A. I was.

Q. Are you acquainted with Llewellyn Banks and his wife Edith Banks?

A. I am.

Q. Will you relate, commencing at the beginning, what that day was and what transpired, and be careful in telling your story, don't tell any hearsay testimony.

A. At about ten-twenty five, or ten-thirty, a telephone call was received at the district office at Medford giving information that Officer Prescott had been shot and requesting assistance. I immediately notified Chief of Police McCredie and instructed the lieutenant to proceed to the place requested at once and to send someone back with the details of all of the happenings.

Twenty minutes later I received a telephone call. I took the phone, giving my name and stating who I was, and Mrs. Banks stated that Mr. Banks desired to surrender to Sheriff Schermerhorn or Deputy Sheriff Lowd if they could be located. She said, "Wait just a moment". Evidently she was speaking to someone else. She said that Mr. Banks would surrender to me personally if I would come to the house if he could be confined to the Jackson County Jail. I advised her that I was not in a position to make any promises of that type and that unless steps were taken to make an immediate surrender that we would be forced to take action to apprehend and thereby endanger anyone in the building. I was informed that if I would come personally to the residence of L. A. Banks that he would surrender. I left at once and just as I was leaving the building Deputy Sheriff Lowd drove up and asked me where I was going. I told him to get in and I would tell him on the way. We proceeded at once to the residence and there was a considerable crowd there and confusion, and parked the car directly in front of the house. Sheriff Lowd assisted the person in charge of the wagon. He helped with the stretcher, assisting the coroner, I assume.

Q. What did you see on the front porch?

A. There were several people standing there as I went up to the door. I caught a fleeting glance of the body lying on my right as I went up to the door. As I stepped up to the door Deputy Sheriff Lowd pointed or drew my attention to the two letters that were lying on a mat directly in front of the door.

Q. I hand you State's Exhibit A-29 and ask you whether that was one of

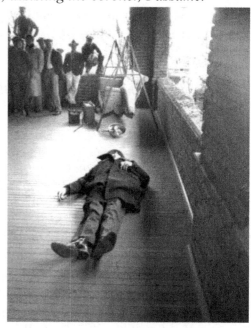

Prescott's body on front porch
Photo from the Southern Oregon Historical Society collection

the letters you found at the door.

A. This was the letter that was lying face up on the mat and addressed to me. That was the envelope.

Q. All right now. Go ahead. Proceed with your story.

A. I picked up those letters at that time, noticing that one was addressed to me, and immediately knocked upon the door of the residence of L.A. Banks. Someone, a lady, looked through the window, noticing who I was. I again knocked and the door was opened. Prior to the opening of the door I heard what I thought at that time was a bolt or lock being opened. Later upon entering the house, before leaving, I discovered it was a burglar chain. Upon entering the house my first question of Mrs. Banks was: Where was Mr. Banks? She merely turned and nodded towards a room to the rear that I assumed to be the dining room. I at once started towards that, noticing Mr. Banks standing there and he started towards me. Mr. Lowd had followed me in and had stepped to the left a little and was holding some conversation with Mrs. Banks that I did not hear. As soon as Mr. Banks entered the room, the main room, he says, "Is this Captain Bown?" I answered in the affirmative and extended my hand and shaking hands with him, walking over to where he was, he at that time walking right towards me nodding towards the front door and stating, "That man tried to break into my house; he tried to force his way right past Mrs. Banks and I shot him." About that time Deputy Sheriff Lowd stepped up and we started towards the front door. At that time Mr. Banks was dressed, had on his hat, wearing his glasses, in an overcoat and had on golf socks. In shaking hands with me he removed his right hand. His left hand still remained in his coat pocket. Just about the time we reached the middle of the room I asked him what he had in his left hand, a gun? He stated, "No, if I did I might be tempted to use it." At that time Mrs. Banks requested permission to send with him some clothing and personal effects. That request was denied on the ground that I didn't want to wait; I was in a hurry. She then wanted to know where he was being taken. I told her I did not know. She asked me if I would advise her. I told her I would. Mr. Banks stated

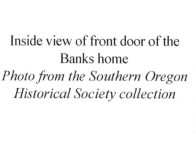

Inside view of front door of the
Banks home
*Photo from the Southern Oregon
Historical Society collection*

to her, *"Everything will be all right, dear, don't worry." And just
before leaving the house I lightly felt of his pockets and waistline
to see if there were any firearms concealed on his person.*

Q. Did you find any?

A. None.

Q. Go ahead.

*A. We left immediately and I was on Mr. Banks left. Mr. Lowd was
on his right. Upon leaving the house we went directly to the car
in front of the house with Officer Pewther driving. The door was
opened by someone and we hurriedly entered the car and left. We
proceeded to the Pacific Highway and then on to Grants Pass.
There was not much said on the ride until about the city limits Mr.
Lowd asked Mr. Banks if there was one shot fired or more than one
shot was fired. Mr. Banks stating, "No, I fired only one shot." He
then was asked if he used the .44 or the rifle. He said he used the
30.06 Newton" At that time Mr. Banks reached in his right hand
coat pocket and brought forth six 30-06 shells, handing them to
me, stating, "I guess I will have no further use for these." I took*

the shells and placed them in my pocket. At about that time Mr. Banks wanted to know if I had the two letters. I stated that I did. I brought them forth from my pocket and the one that was addressed to me I opened it at that time at Mr. Banks request and read it, asking him—

Q. Yes. I will ask you whether State's Exhibit A-20 and 21 respectively is the envelope and letter that you are just referring to.

A. Yes, this is the letter that I read to him, asking him if that was his signature, which he stated that it was and that his wife had written this letter that morning at his request. That a copy of this letter would be found on a table in his residence, and that the other letter addressed to Chief McCredie was an exact duplicate.

Mr. Moody: *I will now offer the same in evidence.*

Q. Continue.

A. Deputy Sheriff Lowd then asked him if he knew that he hit the door. He seemed surprised and said, "I didn't know I hit the door."

There was an interruption in the travel and the subject went back to rifles and guns. He stated that he had purchased this 30.06 while in California for the purpose of hunting mountain lions in the Sierras. He asked me why George Prescott had been sent to serve the warrant. I advised him that the warrants were directed to Constable Prescott and that it was his duty to serve them. Deputy Sheriff Lowd then asked him if the same thing would have happened had himself or myself or Schermerhorn or any other officer come to serve that warrant. He said, "It probably would". He stated there was a burglar chain on the door; that when Prescott came to the door Mrs. Banks opened the door some four or five inches and handed these letters out. That had Prescott taken those letters and gone away this would not have happened but Prescott put his foot in the door and tried to force his way in. That he hollered at him three or four times and he refused to stop but insisted on forcing his way through the door the same as any other burglar would do and that he shot him. He asked me who the young gentleman was with the dark suit on, the younger man with Prescott. I told him

I did not know unless it was Sergeant O'Brien, as I did not know definitely who had gone with him. He said he could have killed him too, "had I wanted to." I believe at that time that he asked for a cigarette. That the conversation went to the different brands of cigarettes that he preferred and which he liked and he at that time told me that he smoked Old Golds, preferred them.

The further conversation, it was mentioned that that morning he had received telephone calls advising him that the warrants, that the grand jury had returned indictments and that five or six secret indictments had been returned and that they were certain that his name was among these. He stated that he had a premonition that morning that something was going to happen. That prior to the arrival of the officers that he had sent Janet away, and I asked him who Janet was and he said that Janet was his private secretary. He asked Deputy Sheriff Lowd if he would do him a favor and he took from his billfold five dollars, a two dollar bill and three one dollar bills, stating that money was hard to get and that Mrs. Banks had very little money in the house, and asked Deputy Sheriff Lowd to take this money and give it to her, which he agreed to do and it was later given to Mrs. Banks. He asked me if I could see that he had a clean place where we were taking him. I told him that the jail at Grants Pass was new and I knew it was clean and doubtless he would be given an individual cell and that he would receive that consideration.

Upon arriving at Grants Pass he was thoroughly searched. His personal effects, part of them, were left with the jailer of Grants Pass or Josephine County and some of them I returned to Medford.

Q. What was Mr. Banks' demeanor during the incidents that he related to you?

A. Very cool, collected, apparently at ease.

Q. Did he seem talkative?

A. Yes.

Q. Did you ever have any subsequent conversations with Mr. Banks?

A. Yes.

Q. When?

A. If I am correct I believe it was two days later in the jail at Grants Pass. Deputy Sheriff Lowd was with me.

Q. Relate it.

A. He said "I am glad that you came down; I wanted to talk with you; there are several things that I wanted to talk over with you." and he proceeded to carry on a conversation without questioning. He stated that his attorneys had been there that day and had talked with him and that they had advised him that Mrs. Banks was in custody. He was somewhat surprised at this, as he did not feel that she should have been arrested. He went on farther to say that he had heard the newspaper boys who were on the street calling out their stories as they often do stating that, "L.A. Banks killed Prescott". He said "Gentlemen, that is not true. When the time comes I will prove who fired the shot that killed Prescott. There was a third man in that house; that he left prior to your arrival, going out the Peach Street entrance and mingling with the crowd and that when we left there I saw him on the corner of Peach and Main streets." He said "When the time comes I will name that man and prove who fired the shot and you remember during our conversation that I said 'when the shot was fired," not 'When I fired the shot.'" He also talked and stated that if we would go to his house we would find the suitcase which was packed with clothing containing a pair of high-topped boots, a canvas coat and other articles and that he knew of this warrant which was being issued or had been warned of it; that he was preparing to leave to go up on Forest Creek to a mine. That Mr. Geiger had been there some time previous and that he had completed arrangements whereby he could go to this mine and that had it not been for the delays and the interruptions that morning and the fact that Mrs. Banks was using the car he would have been gone prior to the arrival of Prescott. He stated that this man whom he would name at a later date had been in his employ; had been hired to do some work; that he had been with him some little

121

time, and that he had also hired Dr. Reddy of Medford to do some work.

He inquired as to where his daughter was and her condition. I assured him she was being well taken care of, being with his brother in-law, Mr. Ward. And also asked to the condition of his wife and at the time requested me to take a note to her which I did, delivering it to her in the Jackson County jail upon my return.

Q. Now calling your attention, in one of the other of these two different series of conversations did he say anything about a card that Mrs. –

A. Yes, that was in the second conversation we had with him.

Q. What did he say about that?

A. He mentioned that a card was passed out and that Mrs. Banks wrote that card at his direction. He thought it was written on the back of a blotter but was not sure.

(Then technical references were made to the State's Exhibits and their admissibility. This led up to the noon recess. After the recess Mr. Lonergan began his cross-examination of Lee M. Bown, state police captain.)

Q. As far as Lumsden and Warren accompanying Prescott and O'Brien to the Banks home, you didn't know they were out there until later, did you?

A. Not until later, no, sir, I did not. I rather anticipated they would be there from the previous conversation and request for assistance.

Q. You knew, did you not, Captain Bown that Prescott had made threats against Mr. Banks?

A. No sir, I did not.

Q. You had heard that rumor hadn't you?

A. No, sir, I had not.

Q. You knew Prescott?

A. I knew Prescott very well.

Q. Yes, and you say now that you did not know that he had threatened Mr. Banks' life?

A. I do. I knew of no threats.

Q. Do you know Joe Cave down there?

A. I know Joe Cave very well.

Q. You knew he had made threats against Mr. Banks?

Mr. Moody: *Object to that, if you Honor pleases, as incompetent, irrelevant and immaterial.*

The Court: *Objection sustained. Not cross –examination.*

Mr. Lonergan: *Q. Are you acquainted with Mr. Walker who is connected with the state police? He also threatened Mr. Banks.*

Mr. Moody: *I object, if you Honor pleases.*

The Court: *That isn't cross-examination. Objection sustained.*

Mr. Lonergan: *Q. Now Mr. Bown, I will ask you whether or not in your conversation with Mr. Banks at the jail at Grants Pass that you didn't tell Mr. Banks that you knew about Prescott and Walker making threats?*

A. No, sir, I made no mention of Prescott and Walker making any threats. I mentioned to Mr. Banks as a possible explanation as to why he was taken to Grants Pass was the attitude of the crowd immediately following the shooting and the attitude at the house.

Q. In that connection did you not say to him that you knew that Prescott and Walker had made threats against the life of Mr. Banks.?

A. No, sir I made no such statements.

On further examination defense tried to attribute Captain Bown knew of threatening statements. Bown claimed he had never heard those statements. The defense chose another tack, returning to when Bown came to Banks' house on the 16th.

Q. And he shook hands with you?

A. Yes, he extended his hand and I accepted it.

Q. And sometime shortly thereafter I believe you said that you asked him something about whether or not he had a gun in his pocket?

A. I did.

Q. Were those the exact words?

A. I asked him what he had in his left hand pocket? A gun? I made the inference.

Q. And the language that was used by you was "what have you in your left hand pocket? A gun?" is that it?

A. Yes.

Q. And he replied to you he didn't have a gun?

A. He said, "No, if I had I might be tempted to use it."

Q. And that conversation took place there in the dining room?

A. No, nearer the door.

Q. He had walked out towards the living room by that time?

A. Yes, we had walked out to the living rom and near the door.

Q. At that very time Captain, when you claim this statement was made by Mr. Banks, just within a very short distance of him on a table I believe you testified there was lying a rifle and a revolver, both of which were loaded?

A. I didn't know they were loaded at that time. They later proved to be.

Q. And they were within very easy access and within very easy reach of Mr. Banks where he was when you first saw him as you entered the house?

A. He could have reached them, yes.

Q. Very easily?

A. He could.

The Court: *It is noon Mr. Lonergan.*

Mr. Lonergan: *Yes, that's right.*

(After the noon recess Mr. Lonergan resumed his cross-examination.)

Q. You delivered Mr. Banks over to the sheriff of Josephine County?

A. I delivered him to the jailer of Josephine County and also left two men to assist the jailer should he need it.

Q. Who was left there?

A. At that time I left Officer Pewther and Officer Folsom.

Q. Where did you meet up with Folsom?

A. Folsom and Taylor I had previously arranged to meet me at the edge of the city.

Q. Grants Pass, you mean?

A. No, at Medford. They met us near Central Point and to act as a convoy and escort if we had car trouble.

Q. They were traveling in an automobile?

A. In separate cars. They were our patrolmen. I had given instruction for Officer Taylor to proceed to Grants Pass and contact us, and Officer Folsom to wait for us.

Q. They met you on the highway you say somewhere near Central Point?

A. Near Central Point.

Q. One of the officers drove ahead of your car, and another behind you is that it?

A. Yes, one preceded and the other followed.

Q. As you drove up to Grants Pass in the car you were not inter-rupted by anybody?

A. No, sir, nothing but just ordinary traffic and stock on the highway.

Q. Now, you have spoken with reference to your conversation with Mr. Banks when you went to Grants Pass the second time, which you say was about the 18th of March in the evening. Was there not some conversation between you and Mr. Banks with reference to Mr. Prescott, which has not yet been stated here? I want to direct your attention particularly to the fact as to whether or not Mr. Banks did not in the course of the conversation with you relate to you the fact that Mr. Prescott had caused him to be indicted for libel?

A. Now I recall that some conversation was had with reference to Mr. Prescott having seized some paper from his news office and the result of an article published by Mr. Banks that he was indicted. I believe for calling him a "bandit," if I remember the conversation rightly.

Q. And Mr. Banks referred to that at the time that you were visiting him there on the 18th of March in the jail at Grants Pass?

A. I recall that he mentioned it, yes, sir.

Q. That Prescott had gone into his newspaper establishment in Medford and taken away a number of bundles of paper?

A. Yes, sir.

Q. And that Mr. Banks had referred to him in his paper as "a ban-dit" and Prescott had had him indicted for criminal libel? I don't know that that is the exact words but that is the substance of it?

A. I do not recall him stating that Prescott had caused him to be indicted, but that he had been indicted.

Q. Didn't he say it was on the complaint of George Prescott?

A. He said that the article that he published in the paper relative to

Prescott was the cause of his indictment.

Q. How long was Banks kept in Grants Pass?

A. I don't recall the exact days. I would say approximately two weeks, somewhere in that neighborhood.

Q. And then what happened?

A. He was returned to the Jackson County Jail.

Q. And then he was kept in the county jail in Medford until he was brought to Eugene for his trial, is that it?

A. To the best of my knowledge, yes.

Q. You were not present, as I understand it, when Mrs. Banks was placed under arrest?

A. I was not.

Q. When you and deputy sheriff went to the Banks home that morning of the 16th, as I understand you testimony, Mr. and Mrs. Banks were the only ones that you saw in the Banks home?

A. They were the only persons we saw inside the house.

Q. And you and the deputy sheriff took Mr. Banks into custody but didn't do anything with reference to Mrs. Banks at all?

A. No, sir.

Q. I suppose then, that you learned about her being in custody after you returned from Grants Pass?

A. After I returned from Grants Pass.

Q. At that time she was placed in the city jail at Medford?

A. Upon my return from Grants Pass she was already in the city jail.

Q. You say that Mr. Prescott as constable of the Medford precinct was also a city policeman?

A. He was employed by the city, yes. He is a traffic officer, I be-

lieve. I am not thoroughly familiar with the arrangement but he operated as city traffic officer.

Q. He was constable as well as city policeman?

A. To the best of my knowledge, yes, sir.

Q. And worked out of the office of the city police at Medford?

A. He was under the supervision of the chief of police, yes.

Q. Do you know whether he wore a constable's badge or city police badge?

A. He wore on his cap emblem, I recall, "Traffic", the word "traffic" on his cap emblem, but as to his star I don't know what it was.

Q. He didn't have "Constable" on his cap?

A. I don't recall it, if it was there. It could be there but I don't recall it.

REDIRECT-EXAMINATION by Mr. Moody:

Q. How tall was Mr. Prescott?

A. I don't know his exact height. Mr. Prescott was very near my height. I happen to know, one evening Officer Sloneker, of the city police department, and myself were arguing about height and we stood up against the wall and marked it off, and Mr. Prescott was either a little taller or a little shorter than I am. I don't recall the exact height.

Q. About your height?

A. About my height.

RECROSS-EXAMINATION BY Mr. Lonergan:

Q. How tall are you?

A. I think I am five ten and three quarters, to be exact.

(Witness excused.)

(The prosecution tried once again to get the "Daddy" note admitted as evidence.)

Mr. Moody: If the Court pleases, at this time I want to, without entering into an extended argument, I want to offer State's exhibit A-11.

The Court: Is that the "Daddy" note?

Mr. Moody: Yes.

The Court: I have ruled on that twice, and I am not going to rule again.

Mr. Moody: I wish to call your Honor's attention to a decision, if the Court please.

The Court: I have ruled on that and I don't propose to change my ruling.

Mr. Moody: All right.

The Court: I have ruled on it twice and held it to be incompetent, and I will adhere to my ruling.

Mr. Moody: The State rests. (Its case)

At 2:45 pm on Thursday May 11, 1933 the state had introduced most of its evidence. A short recess was called. Without the jury present, the defense asked to have the case against Edith Banks dismissed "on the ground that there is no evidence in the case which would warrant a jury in finding a verdict of guilty against Edith Banks…. and that the relationship of husband and wife existed between the defendants and that under the law there could be no conspiracy between husband and wife; on the further ground that there is no showing that there was any criminal intent on the part of the defendant Edith Banks….which directly or indirectly culminated in the death of George Prescott."

To give himself time to consider the defense's motion, Judge Skipworth adjourned the court proceedings until Friday morning at 9:30 a.m.

May 12, 1933

On May 12th the case continued, and while the jury was absent the judge discussed the defense's motion.

The Court: *The court feels very deeply the responsibility that is placed upon it in passing upon this motion, particularly in view of the gravity of the crime charged. In passing upon this motion it is not for the Court to pass upon the guilt or innocence of Mrs. Banks. That is the exclusive province of the jury. The question for the Court to determine under the authorities is: Is there any evidence in this case to go to the jury connecting the defendant with the commission of the crime?*

And the Court, taking the case as a whole, is bound under the authorities and under my view of this case, to overrule this motion. We will now take a recess.

At the end of the recess the jury returned to its box and the case proceeded.

The Court: *I will pass on the motion. The motion for a directed verdict as to the defendant Llewellyn A. Banks is overruled.*

Mr. Lonergan: *Exceptions, please.*

The Court: *Take your exception. The motion for a directed verdict as to the defendant Edith Banks is overruled.*

Mr. Lonergan: *Exceptions, please.*

The Court: *Take your exception. You may call your first witness.*

Mr. Lonergan: *I will call Llewellyn A Banks.*

The crammed courtroom seemed stunned and gasped at the defense tactic of calling Llewellyn A. Banks as its first witness. The 62-year-old, bespectacled Mr. Banks, with silvery gray hair, was impeccably dressed in a gray suit, with matching vest, blue tie and a blue handkerchief in upper left pocket. He looked nervous when he first took the stand, and stared at the floor. Perhaps he was uneasy because the prosecution had recently asserted that he was "a coward, hiding behind a woman's skirts." After a few questions, however, he lifted his head and began his life's story in a soft voice. As he warmed up his voice increased in volume and at times he showed a touch of anger or stood to make a dramatic point.

Both the defense and prosecution had psychiatrists in the courtroom to hear the Banks' testimony. They were there to evaluate if Banks was sane or insane. It tipped off journalists as to the plea the defense planned on using.

Mr. Lonergan: *How old are you, Mr. Banks?*

A. Sixty-two.

Q. Where were you born?

A. I was born at Catawba Island, Ohio, August 15, 1870. My father, formerly a New Englander, a descendant from the Mayflower, was justice of the peace. He held this office from my earliest recollection until he died when I was seventeen years old. My father had a large family, nine in the family, and he had a small fruit farm. Catawba Island was devoted almost exclusively to fruit culture.

The Dictator

At the age of eighteen Banks left his home for Cleveland, Ohio. After a brief stint as a traveling salesman for a fruit house he returned home and started a small business buying fruit for cash and reselling it for a profit. In 1892 when Banks was 22 years old, he married Florence. They were childless, but later adopted a baby girl, possibly from a surviving family member's spouse whose wife had died at childbirth. Mr. Banks doted on his new adopted daughter, Geraldyn.

By 1908 his small business venture led him to becoming the owner of what he claimed was the largest fruit house in Ohio. In 1909 he decided to move to California, where he also began buying, packing, and selling fruit crops. By 1921 he owned over 800 acres of groves and 5 packing houses. He was well respected by other California orchardists.

Banks knew what type of land was necessary to grow first-rate fruit. When he saw apples and pears from the Rogue River Valley he realized that the area must be ideally suited for fruit production. He decided he had to see this land for himself.

By 1926 Mr. Banks had acquired two packinghouses in Medford and over 600 acres of Jackson County orchard land. He was dividing his time between Medford and Riverside in southern California. The stress of maintaining and managing these interests may well have affected his home life. His first wife Florence wasn't happy with the marriage. So he and Florence divorced. Shortly thereafter Mr. Banks married his private secretary Edith

Ward of many years and adopted her daughter Ruth Mae as his own.

There may have been another angle to Banks' claim of adoptions. Both daughters could very well have been Banks, conceived in love affairs during of his marriage to Florence—a possible scenario that might have prompted the divorce. Banks' steadfast insistence that the children were not his may have been another lie he characteristically invented. Getting away with this deceit may well have set the stage for bigger lies to come.

His businesses in and around Medford flourished. In September 1929, L.A. Banks was a wealthy orchardist and landowner; it seemed he could do nothing wrong. He and his wife had fine clothes, two homes, and Mr. Banks managed his business driving between Oregon and California in his Cadillac. People looked up to him and respected his business judgment.

In 1929 Mr. Banks struck out in a new direction by purchasing the *Medford Daily News*. He was determined to make his morning paper the best in Jackson County. He purchased a new office on West Main Street. He enlarged the staff, hiring new reporters and editors. He brought in a new Linotype typesetting machine that featured the most legible type obtainable, and added a costly new Ludlow typography machine.

The former owners in their valedictory editorial said of Mr. Banks, "His extensive land holdings and operations in the pear industry of Rogue River valley have made him a conspicuous figure in this city and district. His association with the business and social life has been such as to establish him as a man of the most constructive type. He is a man of vision, willing to back his vision, and highly capable of making dreams come true." In the same paper on the front page Mr. Banks wrote in bold letters: "The *Medford Daily News* stands squarely for a complete separation of government and business."

In 1930 Medford had three newspapers: Banks' *Medford Daily News*, Ruhl's *Medford Mail Tribune*, and a weekly, the *Pacific*

Record Herald. The *Pacific Record Herald* had been founded about 1926 with Earl H. Fehl as editor and publisher. Ashland, 16 miles to the south of Medford, had its own paper the *Ashland Tidings*.

The month after Banks bought his paper, the stock market crashed. Despite the crash, Banks claimed in early 1930, "Today the *Medford Daily News* has a larger circulation than any other newspaper in the Rogue River Valley." Banks had a good staff, so he only occasionally wrote articles or editorials. During the last quarter of the year Banks became dissatisfied enough with the downward economic trend that he decided to run for public office. He launched a campaign as an independent to unseat the popular thirteen-year veteran Republican Senator Charles McNary. Mc-Nary was well liked in Oregon and because of his years of service was influential on important senate committees, that dealt with power, lumber, agriculture, labor and compensation to Oregon for lands used by the federal government. In the U.S. senatorial race there were five candidates: a Republican, McNary; a Democrat, Watkins; and three Independents.

Banks' campaign stressed economic issues. He felt that freight rates were too high and were especially burdensome on agriculture and timber. He thought the Farm Marketing Act placed extra burdens on agriculturists. He also pushed for repeal of the Eighteenth Amendment, which would end Prohibition. So while the country was struggling to find its next move out of the economic crisis, Banks busied himself with his new paper and running for senator.

Banks' missed the deadline to put his campaign's message into the voter's pamphlet, but his campaign office in Portland sent out advertising to newspapers and set up speaking engagements. In Medford, Banks' newspaper advertised his campaign daily. He found a welcome ally in Earl H. Fehl, editor, owner of the weekly *Pacific Record Herald*. Fehl had recently been exonerated in four libel suits, two of which he won in court. Fehl and Banks backed each other in their newspapers. Fehl, in the same election, was running for his fourth try at becoming Medford's mayor.

The *Medford Mail Tribune*'s editor, Robert Ruhl, derided Fehl as "the hardy perennial, who has been running for Mayor for this city since the Neolithic age." Ruhl wrote that, "When Medford faced bankruptcy" Fehl fought every move to right the ship, and when "Medford started a movement for a new water system Fehl fought it."

Banks tried to start off on a friendly note with Ruhl by sending him a letter in May 1930. "May I compliment you on the two editorials. You give expression precisely to my viewpoints that (the republican party) must first purge itself of its own evil tendencies and come back to the foundation where it originated. Very truly yours, Llewellyn Banks." The letter had been typed by Banks' secretary in his office at Suncrest Orchards. It was perhaps the last friendly correspondence Banks would ever send to Robert Ruhl.

After the senate campaign ended November 2, 1930, the two editors, Banks and Fehl, took their defeats for public office personally. As a first try at running for public office, senator at that, Banks did not fare so badly. He didn't come close to his Republican and Democratic contenders but he managed to defeat the two other Independent candidates. Statewide, Banks got 17,488 votes. In Jackson County the vote was 1201 for Banks and 1702 for McNary. Banks blamed his loss on the Oregon press, on Oregon chambers of commerce, and on the fact he hadn't been advised by the Attorney General about the rules for getting his candidacy in the voter's pamphlet. But he wrote that he was satisfied with his effort. Then he apologized for his papers' editorials, which had supported Fehl so strongly. "All bitterness in such campaigns should be unnecessary."

Fehl's loss was bitter. He thought Medford citizens were dividing into two factions: the ins and the outs. Ruhl, part of the ins, championed keeping Medford's water commission intact. It had been performing a useful service to the city. Fehl, part of the outs, had campaigned for closing the water commission and placing its responsibilities with the city council and mayor.

After the election rhetoric was over in December 1930, Banks and Fehl began working together. Banks took over as editor of the *Medford Daily News*, and found himself pitted against Robert Ruhl, a Harvard graduate with years of newspaper experience in Medford. During his first year Banks came up with the idea to run his paper without advertising, thinking his wealth could sustain it. But, the Depression was eating into his wealth, so he soon gave up the idea. Banks was on edge. When the *Mail Tribune* made a sly comment about one of the *Daily News* headlines, he snapped back, "The *Mail Tribune*'s headlines wouldn't even win the booby prize in a freshman journalism class. The *Mail Tribune* is simply making another one of its cowardly attempts to discredit the *Daily News*, a thing it has tried so often to do, purely out of a consuming jealousy."

1931-Tension

Looking for ways to save money in the Depression, Banks launched an editorial campaign charging that fruit packing contracts were unduly harsh on the fruit growers. The contracts, he claimed, placed mortgages on the grower's crops, farm equipment and included liens on their real property. Banks felt his editorial efforts saved the fruit industry thousands. In another editorial campaign he urged Medford taxpayers to save $235,000 by voting no on a bond issue that would install a new sewer plant. The sewage disposal bond issue could wait. Earl Fehl's paper concurred heartily and used the opportunity to make slurs about the *Mail Tribune*. Voters responded by turning down the bond measure.

When the bond issue lost the *Daily News* and *Pacific Record Herald* felt they had scored a last minute touchdown. Meanwhile economic conditions were worsening, hitting the *Mail Tribune* hard. In a letter to his typesetters Ruhl asked them to take a $3 to $4 dollar reduction in pay per week, "immediately," and "that it would be far better for all concerned, to keep the paper's present working force intact, at a slightly reduced scale, rather than to discharge any employees—many with families to support." Then he consolidated Saturday and Sunday issues into a Sunday paper.

Banks' *Daily News* faced troubles of its own when his union workers walked out. Had it not been for his pal, Earl Fehl, the *Daily News* would not have gone to press. But Fehl prepared the type and the paper was published. Banks wrote, "Applications for positions on the *News* commenced to come in via wire, letter and telephone. Inside of forty-eight hours, the *News* was literally swamped with more assistance than it could make use of." Banks attacked the typesetters' union for trying to send *Daily News* advertisers to the *Tribune*. And when someone claimed that the *Daily News'* circulation was only 3,600 papers, Fehl was outraged and responded that he had printed 5000 copies at least on that busy Sunday when the typesetters had walked off the job. Furthermore, Banks claimed that an unidentified man had been asked by the typesetters' union to jimmy the presses at the *Daily News*.

Times were tough for everyone. Found in Robert Ruhl's personal papers were letters written to him from real estate agents suggesting they had cash buyers for town newspapers. At first Ruhl was tempted and investigated them solely because the future of his publication looked in doubt with two daily's fighting for subscriptions. Similar solicitations were sent to Banks' *Daily News* prompting this headline, "*Medford Daily News* Not For Sale."

Editorials about the economic condition were in great demand. Where the *Mail Tribune* discretely confined its editorials to page 3 or 4, the *Daily News* started using the front page. Banks titled it "Once In A While." At first it was once in a while and was always written by Banks. By 1932 the column with Banks' editorial ramblings would run practically everyday. Banks talked more and more about revolution, a desperate situation, adjustments were needed, we have come to a crisis, recklessness and waste in local government, and over taxation. The situation was coming to a showdown, Banks declared. "The gang" was destroying his newspaper by scheming behind his back. In December Banks wrote, "The gang is carrying on their fight. Individuals in Medford who have axes to grind and who have been grinding them for the purpose of destroying the *News*."

As the 1932 election year approached, people wondered if Llewellyn Banks would try for another elective office. And what about his buddy, fellow editor Earl Fehl? Both claimed it was up to the voter to change the current stagnant, miserable conditions. And just how drastic were conditions for Banks? His wealth was dwindling fast. As his business worries increased, so did his column's intensity and length. For Banks everything was at a crisis point. In Jackson county hard times made unemployed voters bitter and receptive to new ideas, no matter how undemocratic.

1932-Taking Sides

Frustration over taxes was growing. A meeting at the Medford armory of county citizens and county officials was held in January to try and do something about the tax burden. Nothing came of it. Banks editorialized, "Taxes are going to be lowered. Do you know why, Messrs. County Court and the rest of you office holders? The people can no longer pay these taxes." Meanwhile mortgage foreclosures continued and sheriff's sales became common. In the midst of this distress, Banks may have suggested to Fehl that he run for Jackson County judge. If they could secure that position and elect a supportive county sheriff and county commissioner, they could take control of running the local government. Earl H. Fehl seized upon the idea. In his *Pacific Record Herald* he announced, "I enter this race fully qualified to render a real service to the people as well as to my Republican party. Taxes on real property must be reduced. I pledge to you my candidacy for County Judge."

A county judge elected for four years, was one of three officials in charge of overseeing the county's business. Along with two elected county commissioners, the judge met on the first Wednesday of each month to decide on issues as county taxes, bridge construction, road repair, the appointment of election officials, and the boundaries of election precincts.

As the Depression deepened, it became more and more difficult to make a living growing fruit. But work was possible building roads, logging in the forests, gardening, catching salmon from the

Rogue River, hunting deer, panning for gold, and bounty hunting for coyotes. In the hinterlands there were stills manufacturing illegal alcohol referred to as moonshine.

Moonshining was dangerous work. In November 1930 during a raid on a moonshine operation on Reese Creek, eight miles from Eagle Creek, a man named Everett Dahack was shot and killed by a Medford policeman. Medford officers along with state officers waited in hiding around a still operation when the four operators showed up. When the men suspected they were being watched they started to flee, and that is when Joe Cave fired off a shot. There may have been other shots also. Eventually three men were arrested and held and the fourth, Dahack was found dead lying next to six barrels of mash.

Fehl's paper, the *Pacific Herald Record* published an article a week later about the incident headlined, "A Call to Arms." In the article Fehl accused Roy Parr as the man responsible for Dahack's death. With scant evidence, Fehl based his article mostly on gossip. Parr sued Fehl and his newspaper for libel. The trial began in Medford in front of circuit court Judge H.D. Norton on March 3, 1932. The defense declared that Fehl's article was written without malice, or special privilege, and for the public good. The plaintiff's lawyer countered that Roy Parr had been seriously defamed. After four days of testimony the jury agreed and awarded Parr $10,000 punitive damages and $5000 in general damages. After the judges reading of the penalty a *Mail Tribune* reporter said the two litigants met in court after the verdict and shook hands. "Well, Parr, You've broke me," Fehl said. "No I didn't," Parr replied, "you broke yourself." Fehl appealed the verdict. After two months Circuit Judge H.D. Norton announced that the jury had been fair and impartial, so he denied Fehl a new trial.

The libel trial of Fehl was the powder keg that set off a series of new accusations. First, Dahack's widow sought out the district attorney asking him to reopen the case. She claimed that one of the convicted moonshiners said a different policeman, Joe Cave, had shot her husband. But district attorney George A. Codding informed her "that there had been a coroner's jury, a justice court preliminary hearing, a regular grand jury, a special grand jury, with a special prosecutor, and special investigation of Governor Meier that had delved into the case, without finding facts warranting arrests or complaints being found."

Another consequence of the libel trial was that Sheriff Ralph G. Jennings closed down the *Pacific Record Herald,* until the $15,000 fine was paid. Fehl complained bitterly that he and his wife had been evicted from the property before the decision for a new trial was ruled upon. But the sheriff said the city was holding the property intact until the final decision by Judge Norton. During the interim Fehl moved to the office of the *Daily News*, where he set up printing his paper on Banks' presses. On March 17, Fehl editorialized, "The surprise order to get out came last Saturday night and reflects the spirit of the Clique that is out to efface this paper from the face of the earth." In the *Daily News* Banks wrote, "The Fehl libel case is not the only case where there is ample evidence of irregularity in our present jury system.

Earl and Electa Fehl
Photo from the Southern Oregon Historical Society collection

The *Medford Daily News* declares that gang politics are in full control in Jackson County and that these gangsters openly boasted of stifling every newspaper publication that dares to oppose them."

Fehl's paper renewed its attack on county officials, writing that Fehl, "has been put out of business, and deprived of a lifetime's earning because he dared to expose and criticize an unwarranted and outrageous killing of a fellow citizen by a bunch of officers armed to the teeth who surrounded a supposed moonshine still and blew off the head of Everett Dahack."

Fehl's picture was prominently displayed above the article. He was still a candidate for Judge of Jackson County.

Whoever won the election of county judge would set up office in a new courthouse. Fehl and other candidates avoided one issue—the construction of the new Jackson County Courthouse. In 1927 the county seat had been moved from Jacksonville to Medford because the new railroad and Pacific Highway bypassed Jacksonville. The new routes went through Medford. An attractive new courthouse with an Art Deco design was planned for Medford's Oakdale Avenue.

By the end of March, 1932 limestone from Indiana arrived for the courthouse exterior. Work on the rooftop jail had been planned and construction of ground floor partitions was underway. In his report to the county court Inspector Porter said practically all the men employed were "bonafide" Jackson County residents.

Meanwhile the *Daily News* continued its attacks especially on creditors and elected leaders. In a confidential letter from a newspaper wire service to Robert Ruhl in May, George Payne asked the editor if he knew of a "trustworthy and courageous attorney," one who wasn't afraid of Banks and his paper's personal attacks. Banks owed Payne some money and was refusing to pay him. This was an indication that Banks' own wealth was eroding.

Surprisingly in the May primary Fehl beat out five other Republicans for Jackson County Judge. Fehl had won the primary by over 300 votes to his nearest competitor. The *Medford Mail Tribune* was so impressed it wrote, "Any man who can be defeated for public office regularly for a decade and wins in the primary is entitled to congratulations. So the *Mail Tribune* doffs its somewhat battered chapeau." In a separate primary race, George R. Prescott beat out Victor Daley for the position of Medford Constable.

The primary victory for Fehl only whetted aspirations of the two collaborating editors for more attacks. The *Daily News* maintained that the district attorney should be thrown out of office for his decision not to have a retrial on the shooting of Dahack, and that it was the district attorney's indictment of Earl Fehl that closed down his paper. Banks feared his paper would be next. "The *Daily News* respectfully urges the citizens of Jackson County to demand the removal of George Codding from the office of district attorney, not at the end of his term, but NOW." Headlines of this type would continue through the month of August. Banks knew if Codding were reelected he would be in office until 1937.

Robert Ruhl took the month off from battling Banks and Fehl to visit his hometown of Rockford, Illinois. He sent back his observations on economic conditions there. Seven banks had failed, in Rockford and 75 percent of the large manufacturing industry had either closed or was running part time. He wrote, "Coming back to the old home town is something like visiting a museum, where you select and classify your own exhibits." In another editorial, "Here's a new idea, repeal prohibition and prohibit automobiles. Without the automobile bootleggers would quit, gunmen would go out of business, and petting parties would vanish. A reign of righteousness, purity, temperance and industry would be with us again." And, "The next time someone remarks, 'Well, well, Bob, can't say you look any younger!' there is going to be some news on the front page of the *Rockford Gazette-Republic* (for a change): Wild west editor runs amok and slays schoolboy pal."

Shortly after Ruhl left on his vacation, a petition began circulating in the rural districts of Jackson County. It was a petition to recall Circuit Court Judge H.D. Norton. —The same judge who

144

had refused a retrial for Earl Fehl. The president of the southern bar association said the recall effort was without, "cause or merit." *Medford Mail Tribune* editors were searching for the person or persons who had instigated the recall petition. None materialized. Ruhl was livid when he found out. He denounced the invisibly led effort, "So, squash this recall petition before it goes any further by not signing it, and avoid having Jackson County heralded throughout the state as a hot bed of dissension and strife." The petition, he added, was "the most flagrant and outrageous abuse of the recall privilege in the history of Southern Oregon."

The recall petition continued to pop up in rural gas stations. Under Oregon law, at that time, recall petitions required approximately 2500 signatures or 25 per cent of the vote cast in the last general election of the counties involved.

When Ruhl returned from his vacation to Illinois he learned that yet another libel suit had been filed against Banks. The new suit alleged that an article Banks had written was "maliciously false and degrading, without investigating its truth or falsity." The

Jackson County Courthouse, c1940
Photo from the Southern Oregon Historical Society collection

Sheriff Clatous McCredie and the "20 millionth" Ford, downtown Medford
Photo from the Southern Oregon Historical Society collection

article had accused a man of "robbing sluice boxes and dynamiting mine dams."

Ruhl's return to Medford also coincided with the completion of the Jackson County courthouse—the same building that would hold the election ballots in its vault room in the next election. On the first day of September, 1932 the courthouse was dedicated with fanfare that included local bands, parades, and statewide dignitaries.

Not long after the dedication ceremony Robert Ruhl was back at work. The *Mail Tribune* wrote, "Earl Fehl, candidate for county judge, accuses Judge H.D. Norton of unfairness in his conduct of a libel case against Fehl, and therefore asks for his recall." Fehl never admitted being behind the recall petition, but he told a crowd at the Medford armory how he had been framed by his friend and neighbor Circuit Judge Norton. This became one of Fehl's main campaign issues, along with lowering taxes and throwing the Medford gang out of power. He campaigned throughout the county with speeches and radio addresses.

In September Banks wrote about a new candidate for the office of county judge, C.E. (Pop) Gates. Banks called Gates the "gang's candidate." Ruhl's paper immediately endorsed Gates over Fehl. Gates had been mayor of Medford for three consecutive terms, bringing the city out of financial crisis. Ruhl claimed that Gates had lowered taxes as well. Gates' candidacy turned the race into a real competition. However, Fehl had already established a strong base of support since deciding to run in February.

On November 8, 1932, the voters decided among many candidates and many issues. Franklin D. Roosevelt, whom Ruhl opposed, got 7, 519 votes to President Hoover's 5,459 in Jackson County and won nationwide. Repeal of Prohibition (opposed by Ruhl) passed in Oregon by 206,619 to 138,775 and won nationally as well. A statewide measure prohibiting commercial fishing on the Rogue River lost 127,445 to 180,527. In Jackson County elections, George Codding won his race for district attorney, and Fehl outscored Gates to be elected Jackson County judge. The next biggest issue in Jackson County was the sheriff's race. There had been five candidates. Neither of the candidates endorsed by the newspapers won. The winner was Gordon L. Schermerhorn. Ralph Jennings, the current sheriff, came in second on a write-in campaign. On hearing of irregularities on some ballots he considered asking for a recount. Meanwhile Constable George Prescott had no one running against him so he was confirmed unanimously as Medford's constable.

Election of new leaders in Jackson County did nothing to ease the severity of the Depression. The Jacksonville bank failed and creditors closed in on L. A. Banks. It seemed every effort by creditors to get their money from Banks was met with a barrage of front page editorials in the *Daily News* pointing out how they were just trying to silence the free press, and that they were in a conspiracy instigated by the "gang." One of the first "conspirators" was a former employee, *Daily News* accountant H.T. Hubbard, demanding back wages. In an article titled, "Hubbard's Treachery," Banks called the man a cheat and suggested he was in cahoots with the gang, trying to ruin Banks. This case was settled out of court with

Hubbard and other employees getting a good percentage of their back wages.

Before the end of the year Lee B. Tuttle, former owner of the *Daily News*, requested a receivership plea to "insure creditors and the publication itself." He had three liens on the equipment, amounting to $3,333.33 each. There were also the suits for foreclosure of mortgages—including two promissory notes secured by Banks' Suncrest Orchards, for $4500 and $2028, and another note for over $4,000 secured by his West Main Street property.

While Banks' creditors were scrambling to get their money, Sheriff Jennings decided to petition for a recount of the ballots for sheriff. The petition claimed the ballots were discarded for three reasons. On some his name had been misspelled. Others had omitted his middle initial. Still others had written just his last name. If these ballots were validated, Jennings would win instead of Schermerhorn. Banks and his paper opposed the recount. The *Mail Tribune* supported it. Circuit Court Judge Skipworth would decide.

In the waning days of December Banks used his editorials to denounce his creditors, support Schermerhorn's election as sheriff, and rage about Fehl losing his paper.

Banks seemed to be tumbling into a pit of no return—that may have led to a drastic personality change.

January 1933-Usurpers

By the start of 1933 Banks and his cohort Fehl were making plans to take over the government of Medford and Jackson County.

Their petition to recall Judge Norton had stalled, so they planned more petition drives. To take control of Jackson County government they needed certain officials to resign or be recalled. Fehl didn't waste any time in his attempt to take control of the courthouse. Normally two elected commissioners and the elected judge would convene to transact county business. But one commissioner had resigned. In a last minute maneuver the outgoing county board appointed R.E. Nealon to replace him. This meant that Fehl the elected judge, Ralph Billings the elected commissioner, and Nealon the appointee were the three county representatives. Judge Fehl was outnumbered.

On January seventh Fehl wrote in a *Daily News* editorial that he did "not recognize the legality of the appointment of Mr. Nealon." Fehl's challenge had no merit, however, because the state attorney general had already confirmed Mr. Nealon's appointment. Meanwhile, Banks decided to support the newly elected sheriff, because he seemed sympathetic to Banks' cause. Banks probably felt much safer with Schermerhorn as sheriff then Ralph Jennings. Next Banks launched an all-out assault on Jackson County's District Attorney George Codding. On January eighth he wrote, "If George Codding's resignation is not made effective before that date (January 12) the *News* will call on the citizens and taxpayers to establish law and order."

On the ninth, the Medford post of the American Legion pledged support to all of Medford's elected officials, and denounced mob violence. The "American Legion does hereby condemn any newspaper, individuals or group in Jackson county that attempt to gain control of the public offices of Jackson County and employ them in furtherance of their own schemes. (We) denounce all practices that tend to bring the courts of this district into disrepute."

The *Oregonian* quoted Banks, with a headline, "American Legion I Call Your Damnable Bluff!" in Banks' next issue of the *Daily News* he invited the citizens of Jackson County to a demonstration to protest, "the complete breakdown of law and order."

On the tenth the *Daily News* announced that a march on the new courthouse would take place on the next day. The *Daily News* claimed state Attorney General I.H. Van Winkle's decision on the appointment of commissioner Nealon was wrong. Banks further stated that former sheriff candidate Zundell would lead the march, and predicted 3000 participates with petitions for the resignation of Codding, Nealon, Billings, and the county clerk George Carter.

The *Mail Tribune* reported on Friday the eleventh that the march had been moved to Saturday. Furthermore Lowell Zundell said all statements in the *Daily News* saying he would lead the march were "absolutely false." Llewellyn Banks responded, "If there is no other leader with sufficient courage to head this demonstration, I offer my services…." When marchers reached the courthouse, petitions would be circulated for the removal of county officials. Earl Fehl and Banks were to be the principal speakers.

On Saturday about 800 people came to see the demonstration on the front steps of the new Jackson County courthouse. Some wore neatly dented fedoras with brims folded down, and others wore fabric caps. Some wore warm woolen coats with the back collars turned up while others wore suits. The spectators represented a wide spectrum of citizens from businessmen and farmers to laborers. The speakers all wore suits, and Llewellyn Banks, bare headed, stood out from the others. From the courthouse steps Fehl and Banks addressed the crowd. At one point commissioner R.E.

Nealon was asked to speak. In his defense he tried to reason with the unruly crowd against the personal editorial attacks that had been made about him, only to be rudely hooted at, "get a rope," "throw him in the river," and "run him out of town."

As the speakers addressed the people, petitioners gathered signatures. Reporters estimated that about 850 people had signed them. Banks read his speech, a reiteration of his editorials, in a loud voice. He ended by almost screaming his denunciation of County District Attorney George Codding.

The large crowd merited a front-page story in the *Oregonian* with photographs of all the principal people and an interview of Banks by reporter Lawrence Barber. The reporter had quickly grasped the idea that the courthouse throng was being led by Banks to gain control of Medford's county government, and realized it was also a battle between Banks' *Daily News* and the *Mail Tribune* edited by Robert Ruhl. He was quick to note that Banks and Fehl were displeased by the appointment of Nealon because it prevented them from naming the successor, which would have given them control of the county court. Banks told the reporter that he intended to start an organization called the "Good Government Congress." Who would lead the new organization? Banks claimed to have no idea, just as he and Fehl hadn't known who was behind the petitions against Jackson County leaders.

On January 18 the Good Government Congress met. They planned to rid the county of "Dishonorable, disloyal, and unpatriotic public servants." Only the Good Government Congress could bring normalcy, justice and recognition of the people's financial injustices, "which under the existing order of things, have passed beyond individual control." In the same *Daily News* column Banks advised his readers to discontinue reading the *Mail Tribune* because it was a "poisonous, falsifying publication." Further he wanted his readers to boycott its advertisers. In the unfavorable economic climate Banks' wild accusations seemed reasonable. He even told his subscribers that he would like to see the state bar association dissolved, and most state judges removed.

Two local groups attempted to fight Banks' accusations in a calm and reasoned fashion. The Jackson County Civic League and the American Legion called a mass meeting to confront the tyranny

---

I hereby subscribe to the principles and accept membership in the Good Government Congress.

Name ....

Address ....

.... Phone ....

JUSTICE OUR AIM

TRUTH OUR WEAPON

PUBLIC EXPOSURE OUR PENALTY

— PREAMBLE —

We, the citizens, property owners, and taxpayers of Jackson County, Oregon, are faced with economic conditions, which under the existing order of things, have passed beyond individual control.

With all industries operating at a loss or definately closed; with the product of our soil being sold at unprecedented losses far below the cost of production; with tax levies National, State and County, ever on the increase and beyond the earning power of our industries and properties to pay; with half of our population destitute and out of employmnt; with foreclosures on property and eviction from our homes being imposed under the law when there is no means of meeting these obligations; with foreclosures for delinquent taxes effecting a large section of our people with conditions unprecedent and of abnormal nature, we find it necessary to form ourselves into an organization for the protection of our lives, our homes and our properties.

We, the "GOOD GOVERNMENT CONGRESS" of Jackson County, Oregon, in view of the foregoing conditions which have become self evident to all the people, provide a Constitution and By-Laws governing this organization.

As an expression of our faith in the fundimental principles which bind us together, we delare and subscribe to the following:

First, we delare our implicit faith in the fundamental principles under which our Democracy was established.

We subscribe to the spirit and to the phraseology of the Declaration of Independence.

We declare our allegiance to the Constitution of these United States, to the Constitutation of the State of Oregon, AND TO ALL JUST LAWS GOVERNING SOCIETY.

Front and back sides of a Good Government Congress membership card
From the Oregon State Archives

of Banks and Fehl. The meeting drew 1500 people. They voted to stand by the county and support the elected county officials.

Banks countered with the announcement in the *Daily News* of the next Good Government Congress meeting on January 23. He wrote, "To be more explicit, the Good Government Congress to be composed of the law abiding citizens becomes a natural living force developed to completely overthrow gang control of our public servants." At the meeting in the new courthouse, 500 or more membership cards were passed out, and it was determined that the Good Government Congress would have one representative in each district of the county. They passed resolutions calling for the resignations of H.D. Norton and George Codding. In an article on January 26 Banks refused to recognize any legal authority that would try to take from him his land holdings or personal properties.

Banks' appeals for relief from creditors hit a rock when on the 27th the *Jacksonville Miner* revealed that Banks had not even paid his young newspaper delivery boys, who were due months of back pay. The *Jacksonville Miner*'s informant bemoaned "the unfairness of a man who hires but does not pay; who drives an expensive Cadillac while his newsies tread the streets with worn-out shoes and wet feet."

On January 29 Banks wrote that twenty civil suits had been filed against him, and that lawyer M.O. Wilkins who had represented him in the past had withdrawn as his legal representative. Wilkins had resigned because Banks had not paid him for his services leaving Banks without any representation. Banks considered all this as revenge against him personally. Fehl was not doing so well either. His wages as county judge were being garnished to pay for his libel lawsuit fines. He called for vengeance and wrote a column asking the citizens of Jackson County to help him out of his financial jam. "I am asking you people to come to my aid. Upon your answer to my request hinges the destiny of every citizen of Jackson County."

As January 1933 came to a close three other events shook Banks' political aspirations. One, Judge George F. Skipworth was expected to rule that there would be a recount of the ballots for sheriffs. Just when Schermerhorn and Banks had cozied up, now even that alliance was in jeopardy. Ralph Jennings was sure he had won. Secondly, L.B. Tuttle was owed $11,000 on promissory notes from Banks for the purchase of *Medford Daily News*. Then came the other shocker. On the 30th the leaders of the Good Government Congress met to appoint officers. Mrs. Henrietta Martin was elected its president and Guy L. Ray elected treasurer. The next day Ray denounced the organization in the *Mail Tribune*. "I cannot subscribe to an institution that supports the Declaration of Independence, and is ruled by a dictatorship." Ray resigned from the Good Government council because Banks had been named the first honorary President, with the power to overrule every decision made by the Congress.

February - Ballot Thefts

The first five days of February unleashed more problems for Banks. A suit was filed in circuit court against Banks' Suncrest Orchards, alleging an unpaid balance of over $2000 for fruit purchased in 1931 and 1932. Banks had also defaulted on payments for the *Medford Daily News'* building. Then Banks' lawyer M.O. Wilkins had a financial grievance too, "failure to obtain compensation for services rendered," approximately $10,000. Banks wrote an editorial saying the lawyer was guilty of extortion, and Wilkins countered by filing a suit for libel.

Justice Roberts issued a warrant for Banks' arrest, and demanded that he appear in the Ashland courthouse on Saturday at 10am. The warrant was given to Sheriff Schermerhorn to enforce. Meanwhile Banks announced that the "First General Assembly" of the Good Government Congress would be held on the same Saturday morning he was supposed to be in court. He wrote, "Only a miracle may be able to prevent wholesale bloodshed in Jackson County." He added, "I will resist to the utmost of my ability any attempt to seize me and take me before this prejudiced court."

On Saturday morning at 10 am in Medford's armory building, Banks addressed the Good Government Congress faithful—a crowd of about 2,000, according to Judge Fehl, but more like 1,200 to 1,500, according to the *Ashland Tidings*. Still, it was a large crowd, and probably included a good share of the *Medford Daily News'* 5,057 subscribers. Banks' speech touched on large issues that might have been appropriate for a candidate for US Senate— introducing new mediums of exchange, denouncing the Federal Banking Reserve, and lowering power rates. He also extolled the crop, lumber, and mining industries of Jackson County. But before positive change could occur, Banks said, "Jackson County must reestablish law and order, and the removal of certain officials from office." Henrietta Martin presided over the meeting and let Mrs. Adah Deakin speak to the crowd. She scolded M.O. Wilkins for filing a libel suit against Banks. This seemed to embolden the crowd in support of Banks. At that point Judge Fehl invited the crowd to attend the Ashland courtroom where Banks was to appear before Judge Roberts at 2pm.

Sheriff Schermerhorn failed to deliver the warrant to Banks as requested by Justice of the Peace Judge Roberts of Ashland. On Saturday, when Banks didn't show up at the prescribed time the judge delayed the hearing to 2pm. Banks finally appeared, along with about 500 cheering members of the Good Government Congress. At one point during the hearing Judge Roberts had to order quiet in the courtroom. Banks' supporters filled the room and paced the sidewalk outside the building. Banks' bond was set at $1000. Six property owners signed Banks' bond. The libel suit would now go to the grand jury to determine if the suit was justified—all within the first five days of February. Banks, Judge Fehl, and the Good Government Congress were certainly turning heads.

On February 8th Gene Wright obtained a writ of attachment on Banks' newsprint. Allison Moulton, Wright's attorney, presented the case to Justice of the Peace Judge Coleman. Coleman approved the writ and Constable Prescott confiscated all the newsprint in the Daily News' office. Judge Coleman would later say, "That paper was not seized illegally, nor was it held illegally." Banks called it an illegal act of "banditry." Banks was able to secure more paper and produce his publication on schedule the next morning. Banks claimed it was because of several patriotic citizens that paper was purchased for him to use. In his front-page column he wrote, "Mr. George Prescott, in full uniform with a badge of authority, seized the paper." Prescott "violated the law with full knowledge of his act." He added, "A state of complete ANARCHY now exists in Jackson County."

Constable Prescott in uniform
Photo from Southern Oregon Historical Society collection

The *Jacksonville Miner* claimed the Good Government Congress was bordering on syndicalism. "Criminal syndicalism is hereby defined to be the doctrine which advocates crime, physical violence, arson, destruction of property, sabotage or other unlawful acts" to take over the existing form of government. The Jacksonville paper noted that the purposes of the Good Government Congress under Banks were three-fold—political, financial, and criminal.

The political goal was to dislodge the district attorney, county clerk George Carter, and commissioners Nealon and Billings through the recall and threats. The financial purpose of the Good Government Congress was to collect membership dues and put this money in Banks' hands. The organization was criminal because secret committees were being formed to use armed force if necessary to remove elected officials. According to one witness, Banks shouted at a February 10th meeting, "The Good Government Congress serves notice on Circuit Judge Norton and DA Codding, that either you will destroy us or we will destroy you."

In a letter written in 1935, Ruhl summed up the effects of the rebellion: "Our circulation at the outset of the campaign was around 4700, it went down to approximately 4000; while the merchants as a whole were behind us, many of them were afraid to advertise, because to do so meant loss of trade. During this period the *Mail Tribune* for the first time in its history went deeply into the red and for a time weekly payrolls could not be met. The Depression of course was partly responsible, but the boycott against the paper was the chief factor. Many citizens went about armed, for Banks had an armed bodyguard of gunmen with him all the time, and a force of armed vigilantes in the hills. I never carried a gun personally, but some men on the paper did, and we had to maintain an armed guard at the plant day and night during the height of the turmoil. We had many anonymous threats, dire warnings, and one or two scares when at night the armed guard discovered suspicious characters around the plant.

Robert Ruhl with golf cap on
Photo from Southern Oregon Historical Society collection

"The difficult part of the entire mess was the fact that the revolution was launched by the editor of a rival paper, L.A. Banks, not a trained newspaper man, but a person of shrewdness, force and ability, who was smart enough to turn everything the *Mail Tribune* said as professional jealously and the desire to drive out a competitor—a counterattack difficult to meet."

Banks' daily newspaper column had selfish aims too—he used it to discredit his creditors so he wouldn't have to pay mounting debts, and to further his ultimate goal of seizing control of Jackson County government. The word "dictator" was not such a harsh word in 1933. Maybe a dictator could get things done, like Hitler in Germany, or Mussolini in Italy. On February 11, Judge Norton advised the Jackson County grand jury that something had to be done about Banks' daily vicious attacks on county officials. Banks' propaganda suggested that law and order had broken down. If the public refused to get involved, just acquiesced, then it should be up to the grand jury to act.

DAILY NOOSE PRINTS PAPER

Above photo, snapped by Staff Photographer Verne Shangle, snows a few of the No Government congress Greenspring mountain boys aiding in getting out the latest edition of the Daily Noose. "Yes, sir, that there newsprint belongs to us, and both barrels will prove it." growled one of the men as he cocked his artillery. "We'll show 'em some law and odor," mumbled another as he eyed the nearest exit.

Jacksonville Minor, Feburary 18, 1933

The *Mail Tribune* commented, "If the statement of Judge Harry D. Norton does not wake up the people of Jackson County to their peril, and to their duty, then we fear nothing CAN! Either we are to have law and order here, either we are to have a community where the courts are upheld, where public officers, whose duty it is to support the law, are supported by the people in the performance of their duty, or we are going to have lawlessness and disorder, a reign of anarchy and terror. An aroused public opinion can clear up this mess, and only an aroused public opinion can do it." The *Dalles Chronicle* wrote, "Fortunately, the Jackson County grand jury has acted to end this "reign of terror, and an effective muzzle soon may be forthcoming for Editor Banks."

By February 19, L.B. Tuttle, former owner of the *Daily News*, was suing Banks and the Medford Publishing Company. Tuttle sought receivership, possession, and the collection of $11,000. If Tuttle won then the *Daily News* would revert to him. Banks would be out. The case would be tried on Friday the 24th. A *Mail Tribune* editorial summed things up, "There can be no economic recovery here, there can be no constructive program realized whether offered by the *News* or any other paper, until the present reign of terror which the *News* alone is responsible for has been put down." The *Jacksonville Miner* ran a photograph of two guards armed with rifles inside the *Medford Daily News* office.

Late on Monday February 20, Banks was indicted by the Jackson County grand jury for libel and criminal syndicalism. Earlier in the day Circuit Judge Skipworth ordered a recount in the sheriff's election, which was a direct challenge to the election of sheriff Schermerhorn. The recount would take place the next day, Tuesday morning. Some claimed the count might even uncover other ballot irregularities. The night before the recount a big meeting of the Good Government Congress was scheduled at the courthouse. The three main speakers were Judge Fehl, President Henrietta Martin, and L.A. Banks. Banks' financial empire was collapsing and government officials were beginning to fight back.

Sometime prior to the February 20 meeting of the Good Government Congress, the conspirators met to decide how to proceed. Attending were Arthur La Dieu, former business manager for Banks' newspaper; Walter Jones, Mayor of Rogue River; John Glenn, jailer at Medford; Thomas Brecheen, political leader from Ashland; Sheriff Gordon Schermerhorn; and Judge Earl Fehl publisher and judge from Medford. Schermerhorn and Fehl feared a recount would expose voting irregularities that would cost them their jobs. These six men decided that the only way to stop a recount was to steal the ballots.

As people were filing in for the Good Government Congress meeting the night of February 20, Judge Fehl huddled with some men in the hallway near the vault room, the room where the ballots were kept. The other men were John Glenn, jailer; Charles Davis, deputy sheriff; Walter Jones, mayor of Rogue River; C.J. Conners, Good Government Congress Vice President; Thomas Brecheen, Good Government Congress member; Also on hand were Mason Sexton, age 19, and his brother Wilbur, 21, and their father. The two brothers were boarding at the jail doing odd jobs for food and room. They were convenient pawns for Fehl and Banks. None in the group had a key to the inside door of the vault room. The outside window to the room, normally protected with a steel shutter, had suspiciously been left un-shuttered.

Before Fehl left to give his speech to the Good Government Congress, the men came to the conclusion that in order to get the ballots they would have to break into the room from the exterior window. Fehl put Walter Jones in charge of the operation. The Sexton brothers were given an important job. They would have to break open the window. John Glenn had told the pair they would get $10 for their work. Fehl was still present when it was decided that the Sextons would use an axe from the tool room to smash open the window. Then Fehl left to deliver his speech.

Judge Fehl had been advised by the grand jury to keep order while the meeting was in progress. Fehl ridiculed the idea of recounting ballots four months after the election. When Mrs. Martin spoke she also criticized Judge Skipworth's decision for a recount. Then L.A. Banks spoke. He asserted that there had been a breakdown of law and order, and a miscarriage of justice. Jackson County's troubles will never be settled peaceably. Then he called on targeted officers of the county to resign.

When the moment came for the break-in to start, the Good Government Congress speakers roused the crowd to laughing and cheering. R.C. Cummings was told to rev up his auto engine as a signal to the Sextons to smash the window. Then C.J Conners, a small man, squeezed through the window into the vault room. He tossed the bags of ballots outside. Cummings took the first load of five bags and drove off. Virgil Edington of Gold Hill loaded the next six bags into an auto. With him were, Wesley McKitrick and La Dieu. Edington later pleaded guilty to the crime. The three drove to the Rogue River mayor's home for instructions. Jones told them to take the ballots to McKitrick's parents' house and burn them in their stove. The Mayor gave them some pitch so that the ballots would burn better. They followed Jones' instructions and burned most of the ballots in the parent's cook stove while the parents watched. Later the parents were witnesses for the prosecution. After the ballots were burned the three men took the empty ballot bags, filled them with rocks, and dropped them into the mouth of Galls Creek. Then the three were to go to Banks' house to solidify an alibi. But Banks' lights were out. After a couple of days Arthur La Dieu approached Edington, saying they needed to get their alibi in order. "We'll go up to the bosses and get straightened out on our alibi." Then the three went to the Banks' house where Mrs. Banks suggested ways the boys should stick by their alibis in a court of law. Mr. Banks said, "I will stand by my boys."

During the nights robbery more ballots were loaded in other cars and some were burned in the countryside.

About fourteen men were involved behind the courthouse, armed with pipes, clubs, and pistols. After the ballot pouches where loaded into the cars, Sheriff Schermerhorn waved to the men as they drove by. When the men returned to the courthouse the Good Government Congress meeting was over and all was quiet. Mr. Breecheen ordered the Sexton brothers to burn the remaining ballots. They burned them in the courthouse basement furnace. The next morning when confronted by sheriff Schermerhorn the boys were ordered to keep their mouths shut.

One the next day, the *Mail Tribune* lamented, *What are we coming to! The courthouse was broken into, the vault was smashed and ballots, cast for sheriff at the last election were stolen! Now we ask the people of Jackson County to whose interest it was that these ballots should be stolen, and this recount dismissed?*

Early Tuesday morning the investigation into who was responsible for the ballot thefts was underway. The *Mail Tribune*, *Ashville Tidings*, and *Jacksonville Miner* all had headlines about the theft. The "Committee of 100" Medford citizens, set out to expand their membership in a conscientious backlash to the Good Government Congress. The Medford Lions Club unanimously advocated for the embattled county officials and offered support to the grand jury. The Jacksonville City Council issued a statement opposing the lawlessness of Banks' followers, endorsing county officials, and they condemned the "false propaganda and false, scurrilous, and libelous statements made in the *Daily News*."

On Thursday morning Banks was charged with syndicalism and libel. Banks, without the benefit of counsel, pleaded not guilty on all charges. On the syndicalism charge District Attorney Codding had already filed for a special prosecutor to investigate the case. The courtroom was filled with Good Government Congress members who remained orderly. Banks was given five days to enter his objections.

The next day Friday in front of Circuit Judge W.N. Duncan of Klamath County, Banks was confronted with two complainants O.B. Waddell demanded payments on overdue loans secured by mortgages on Suncrest Orchards. Lee B. Tuttle, president for receivership, of the News Publishing Company wanted Banks to pay $11,000 on promissory notes. During the morning court session Banks banged his fist on the table. Judge Duncan rebuked him, "This is a court of law. Because one of us loses his head, it is no sign all of us should." Banks stormed out of the courtroom. Afterwards Tuttle's attorney Roberts noted, "Banks made no denial of the debts." Judge Duncan said he would render his decision in a few days.

Meanwhile the state police had arrested the Sexton brothers in connection with the ballot thefts. Based on reliable, but circumstantial evidence, they were held in seclusion. After a few days in isolation the youths confessed, implicating all of the major characters involved in the burglary. Many of the suspects were rounded up on Saturday—even, Sheriff Schermerhorn. He objected, "they've sure got the wrong man this time." Earl Fehl had been tipped off and had left town. The "dictator" himself, Llewellyn Banks had not been charged because he had been crafty and could not be directly implicated.

Also on that Saturday a grand jury indicted Officer Joe Cave for involuntary manslaughter in the killing of Everett Dahack during the 1930 moonshine raid. With testimony from two of the workers at the still and the officers involved in the raid the jury was willing to indict Officer Cave, even though the case had been settled earlier by a county grand jury. Some claimed an errant shot had ricocheted and hit Dahack. In any case Officer Cave would now have to face trial.

On the 13th a decree issued by circuit court Judge W.M. Duncan granted Lee Tuttle immediate possession of the *Daily News*. Already a group of Banks' men known as the "Green Spring Mountain Boys" had begun moving equipment from the site. They were stopped by Sheriff Schermerhorn (now out on bail), along with attorney Gus Newberry and Mr. Tuttle. Tuttle immediately took charge of the newspaper office. The stormy career of Banks' as an editor had finally ended. Mr. Tuttle, "a stickler for the truth," began work as the new publisher of the *Daily News*.

That night people gathered on the streets and sidewalks outside the *Daily News* office. Some were Good Government Congress members; others were just curious. Leonard Hall, publisher of the *Jacksonville Miner* walked into the newspaper office about 6pm for a chat with the news staff. When he left the office, Mrs. Henrietta Martin confronted him, swinging a whip that lashed him across his face. In the scuffle that followed, Mrs. Martin was roughed up a bit and her two male friends took hold of Hall, only to be confronted by the police. Martin, her male friends and Hall were taken to the police office. Hall refused to file charges. Mrs. Martin claimed she had appeared before the grand jury to seek redress about an article Hall had written. When the jury refused to indict Hall she brought a whip to the newspaper office to lash him in public.

On Sunday the 26th there was a new *Daily News*. Under the heading "Announcement" the editor proclaimed, "Today the plant of the *Daily News*, together with all right, privileges and franchises are in the possession and control of the *News* Publishing Company. "The *News* will appear regularly and will follow a news and editorial policy dedicated to upholding law and order through recognized courts and governmental machinery and those public officials who are elected and appointed to administer them."

The new paper was heartily welcomed by the editors of the *Medford Mail Tribune* but they were also cautious.

Under the headline, "Is the "WAR" Over?"Ruhl wrote, *The decision does not rest with the peace-loving and law-abiding citizens of this county; it rests with a small group of unscrupulous politicians, who have so poisoned the minds of the unwary and unsuspecting, that they hope through continual dissension and disorder, to feather their own nests, and literally establish a dictatorship. The next move is up to them.*

On the morning of Monday the 27th a warrant was issued for Judge Fehl. Sergeant O'Brien and Constable Prescott were given the duty of arresting him. It wouldn't be easy because the judge was busy doing his work in the courthouse, and his followers were crowded around him. Just in case, O'Brien and Prescott stashed tear gas bombs in their pockets before going to the courthouse. The arrest proved to be easier than they had thought. After they shouldered and shoved their way through the hostile crowd, Fehl hesitated a moment, but then he resigned himself to arrest when they read the warrant. That same day three of Banks' gunmen were taken into custody. The men had been hired to protect the *News* office.

Many members of the Good Government Congress began to feel as though they had been "used" by Banks. After the ballot thefts many began to turn in their membership cards. They finally understood what the Good Government Congress was trying to do. On closer scrutiny the Good Government Congress was an organization like the KKK, with ulterior motives hidden behind popular and patriotic jargon. The leaders of the Good Government

Congress, Ruhl proclaimed, "were responsible for the most serious threat to orderly government and constituted authority in the history of Southern Oregon."

As the month of February came to an end, police were still making arrests in the ballot theft case. Banks' paper had been shut down on February 20, so he could no longer marshal his troops with editorials. The Good Government Congress had been significantly diminished, but the inner circle remained. The leaders that had been arrested in the theft case were soon out on bail, holding meetings. What were they up too? How would Banks and Fehl reach their Good Government Congress members now that they were without a newspaper?

March - Murder

Fehl had regained control of the *Pacific Herald* newspaper building. He and his wife Electa made arrangements with the new owners of the printing equipment to publish a few more weekly papers. This would also give L.A. Banks another chance to editorialize, so the two conspirators could carry on.

The secretary of the Good Government Congress, C.L. Brown, was the father of the group's president, Henrietta Martin. On his word an article appeared in the new *Pacific Herald* weekly accusing the Farmers and Fruit Growers Bank of illegally sneaking money out of the back door. Authorities at the bank emphatically denied the charges. They charged libel, and a warrant was soon put out for Brown's arrest. Brown had been in the habit of eating free meals at the jail —without proper authorization—but now he skipped town altogether.

Brown's co-conspirator Judge Fehl now out on bail, went back to work at the county courthouse. He wanted the ballot thieves brought before his court, so he could hear the evidence brought against them. He also wanted to free them. Fortunately the men had been moved from the Jackson County jail to Josephine County, out of Judge Fehl's jurisdiction. Fehl angrily made out a warrant for the arrest of Medford's Chief of Police, McCredie. But he couldn't get Sheriff Schermerhorn or anyone else to serve it.

Meanwhile Judge Fehl, Banks, and Henrietta Martin spoke at a Good Government Congress function in Talant, Oregon. They ended their presentation by announcing that another meeting of the Good Government Congress would be held on the steps of the Medford courthouse, at 1:00 p.m. on Monday, March 6.

On March 4, 1933 Franklin D. Roosevelt was inaugurated as the United State's 32nd President.

His speech was broadcast on many radio networks across the nation. Millions heard it, including thousands in Medford and Jackson County. "So, first of all, let me assert my firm belief that the only thing we have to fear is fear itself. Only a foolish optimist can deny the dark realities of the moment. Our greatest primary task is to put people to work. We must act quickly." If congress did not enact his legislation to fight the Depression he would, "ask the Congress for the one remaining instrument to meet the crisis— broad executive power to wage a war against the emergency." The speech was given with commanding oratory. Here was a leader capable of resolving the crisis and inspiring the people.

Meanwhile, back in Jackson County, editorials in the *Ashland Tidings* and the *Mail Tribune* advocated that Fehl and Schermerhorn step down or resign. Even with new hope blossoming nationally, and increased criticisms locally, Banks, Fehl and Henrietta Martin carried on the Good Government Congress.

On the courthouse steps at 1:00 p.m., approximately 1,000 people showed for the Good Government Congress meeting. The main speakers were Mrs. Henrietta Martin, Judge Fehl, and L. A. Banks. They brought the same tired accusations. Mrs. Martin said the stolen ballots "never should have been counted owing to the condition they were in and should have been destroyed months ago." When Banks spoke, he said the government gang had taken $200,000 and his paper from him. He vowed, "Unless justice is restored, I will take to the field—take the field in revolution."

Of course those words caused quite a stir in the papers. The articles also reported that Mrs. Martin felt she was justified in striking the Jacksonville editor with her whip because the grand jury wouldn't recognize her claim against the editor. "I had to do it," she said. The *Mail Tribune* responded, "Mrs. Martin says she has the right. The law says the grand Jury has the right. Good Government? What an absurdity!"

The Good Government Congress had planned a meeting for Prospect, Oregon, but had to cancel when the school board rescinded its earlier decision to let Judge Fehl speak in the school gymnasium. Evidently the board had been unaware that Banks was to speak. When they found out they changed their minds. Following this rejection the group spoke at Shady Cove to a group of over 100 people. A reporter remarked that L.A. Banks had a style of speaking that was inflammatory and "apt to incite people to violence and bloodshed." The Good Government Congress leaders next spoke in Wimer on March 10. There the state police arrested R.C. Cummings, as one of the men involved with ballot thefts.

The leaders of the Good Government Congress next hoped to meet with the Governor in Salem, and then hold a meeting at the Medford armory. But the governor never showed up for their scheduled meeting, and the attorney general refused their use of the Medford armory. Meanwhile the state's case against the ballot thieves grew tighter, as more people were arrested. The information that was collected was referred to as "startling." The people who had been congregating at the new courthouse were suddenly not there anymore. Peace was returning to Medford. Renunciations of Good Government Congress memberships cards were coming in thick and fast.

On March 13, Fehl asked Good Government Congress members for funds to help buy the *Medford Daily News*. The remaining assets of the newspaper were to be auctioned off on Wednesday the 15th. Fehl said the funds would be used to reestablish the free press in Jackson County. Fehl also encouraged people to protest the sale. Both Banks and Fehl were issued restraining orders not to interfere with the auction. On the morning of the 15th Sheriff Schermerhorn conducted the sale. He stood on an office chair and called for bids, but he could only coax one offer, for $6,300. It came from the original owner and founder of the newspaper, L.B. Tuttle. Many Good Government Congress members showed up but after the sale

Banks' supporters dispersed. Banks and Fehl were nowhere to be seen.

Meanwhile the state police had arrested Wesley McKitrick, a close associate of Banks. McKitrick confessed to a plot that Banks had hatched to kidnap the government's elected leaders. The conspirators would have taken Codding and Norton into the woods and strung them up. With this evidence a warrant was finally approved for the arrest of the grand leader, the dictator L.A. Banks.

Banks was at the end of his reign, confronted with indictments, the loss of his agricultural properties, the foreclosure of his house, the loss of his paper, and the flight of members from the Good Government Congress. Someone gave him a tip that a warrant for his arrest was imminent. Banks prepared to leave town, or to shoot the first officer that dared enter his home. He readied a high-powered rifle, loaded his revolver, and stockpiled additional ammo and weapons.

Sergeant O'Brien and Constable Prescott prepared to serve the warrant against Banks on the morning of March 16. Before they left, Prescott made a quick visit to his ailing wife. She was bedridden with a nervous breakdown from all the lies that had been put in the *Daily News*. When he returned from seeing his wife Constable Prescott took the warrant and got in a police car with Sergeant O'Brien. Officers Warren and Lumsden followed in another police car, ready to take up a position in the back of the house incase Banks tried to flee.

Prescott and O'Brien arrived at the front of the house at 1000 West Main Street just as the others got into position. The two officers quickly walked up the path and steps to the front door. O'Brien knocked. They waited tensely for at least a minute. O'Brien knocked again. Then he heard the burglar chain being dropped in place. Mrs. Banks opened the door slowly the length of the chain. Prescott said, "I am sorry Mrs. Banks but we have a warrant for-----". Looking through the door window O'Brien saw Banks with the rifle leveled on his shoulder, aimed at the front door. O'Brien claimed Banks shouted "All right" to his wife and fired a shot. Constable Prescott was never able to finish his sentence. O'Brien tried to move Prescott out of the way but was too late. The bullet killed Prescott on impact. His warrant dropped to the porch floor covered with Officer Prescott's blood.

Prescott's Funeral

After the shooting, Constable Prescott's body was moved to Conger's Funeral Parlor, and a funeral was set for March 19th.

During the period between Prescott's death and his funeral, the rebellion Banks had hoped for did not happen, but the killing left Medford in turmoil. State police officers patrolled the streets and guarded the houses of threatened county officials. One of Banks' supporters was beaten so bad he had to be hospitalized. The state police disbanded a crowd of people that had met at the Medford armory wanting revenge for the death of Prescott.

On the 19th of March the newspapers covered the funeral of George J. Prescott. He was born at Rockford, Illinois on October 4, 1870. At the age of three he with his parents and siblings moved to Bagley, Iowa. While still in Bagly he married Lottie Ford. From Bagley the Prescott family moved to Belgrade, Montana in 1906. Prescott served there as chief of police and later as a deputy sheriff. Next came a position in Denver working for a juvenile court. Finally in 1920 the family moved to Medford. Since that time he had been a city police officer.

There were three surviving children: Francis Prescott of Klamath Falls, Paul Prescott of Medford, and Mrs. Nota Henderson of Salem. Prescott also had several brothers and sisters that lived out of the county.

Prescott had been very involved with-in the community. He had held every elected position in the local chapter of the Independent Order of Odd Fellows (IOOF), a national service organization. He belonged to the Modern Woodmen, a fraternal life insurance company, and the Lions club, an organization for community betterment. He also held a management job for the local Boy Scouts of America.

More than 4,000 people flooded to his funeral on that Sunday afternoon. The Medford armory only had space for about three thousand people, so others waited outside. Still others lined the streets for the procession that would take Prescott's body to the IOOF cemetery. The funeral was said to have been the largest ever held in Medford.

On the stage in the armory sat Prescott's casket, and behind that was a huge American flag on the wall. Legionnaires lined the aisles. As the procession moved to the street, people stood at attention watching the hearse drive by to the I.O.O.F. Eastwood Cemetery.

In his bid for power, L.A. Banks had made a serious miscalculation when he shot such a popular police officer. A serious question remained: was Llewellyn A. Banks sane?

Trial's End

While on the witness stand Banks claimed he had been framed in the ballot theft case and thought the warrant for his arrest had been rigged. Then he raged that many threats had been made against his life. He named three men that his associates had said would shoot him on sight: George Prescott, officer Joe Cave, and a state police officer by the name of Walker. Walker and Cave were a part of the prosecution case. Banks felt that he had been threatened so many times he thought it was necessary to have bodyguards, a guard at his newspaper's office, and a guard chaperoning him to Good Government Congress meetings. During the shooting on Banks' front porch a few witnesses maintained they had seen a gun in Constable Prescott's hand as he fell to the porch floor. In his testimony Banks said, "I saw what I believed to be a pistol" in the Constable's hand. Sergeant O'Brien adamantly maintained that Prescott did not draw his weapon.

The witnesses who heard accusations that Prescott would kill Banks proved to be Good Government Congress members and in most cases unable to prove their claims. Judge Fehl's, for example, claimed Prescott told him he would kill Banks. But, Fehl had no witnesses to verify his story.

Banks had been testifying for a long time, perhaps eight hours, when Mr. Moody began his cross-examination. It took 15 minutes at the most, asking unimportant questions, and then Mr. Moody abruptly dismissed him.

This was a clever move, demonstrating that the state was prosecuting Banks—not persecuting him.

Nevertheless the defense felt Banks was being threatened, Mr. Lonergan also claimed that Banks was not sane at the time of the shooting. He presented two psychiatrists to back up that claim. This brought about another interesting set of witnesses both for the defense and the prosecution.

DIRECT-EXAMINATION by Mr. Lonergan:

Q. Would you state your name, please?

A. S.E. Josephi.

Q. Where do you live, Doctor?

A. Portland, Oregon.

Q. Are you a graduate of a recognized and reputable school of medicine and surgery?

A. I am.

Q. You have been practicing your profession in Oregon for how long?

A. About fifty-five years.

Q. Have you specialized at all in the profession?

A. I have. I have specialized in nervous and mental diseases.

Q. Doctor, did you have occasion to meet Llewellyn A. Banks, since this trial began?

A. I have, yes.

Q. You had never known him prior to that?

A. I had not.

Q. Did you have any occasion to talk with him and examine him in his cell in the jail in this county?

A. I did. I examined him for a period of two to three hours.

Q. Were you accompanied at that time by any other professional man, or doctor, I mean?

A. I was, Doctor Scaife.

Q. I shall ask you then, doctor, as a result of your examination of Banks, and the observations that you made of him, and the hearing of the testimony that was given by him from the witness stand, and assuming those statements to be true, what is your opinion as to whether or not on the 16th of March, 1933, at the time of the shooting of Prescott, the defendant Banks was sane or insane?

A. At the time of the shooting my opinion is that he was insane. That he was affected with what is known by some authorities as transitory mania, and by other authorities as compulsory or impulsive mania, and by other authorities as mental confusion. I will state in explanation that some authorities demur to the use of the term "transitory mania" as applied to the condition that I think this man was in at the time, because it is apt to be confounded with a term known as "acute delirious mania", which is a different condition entirely, and a very fatal condition. Whereas transitory mania, or compulsive or impulsive insanity or mania is a transitory condition which is not fatal and which passes off quickly.

Mr. Lonergan: You may cross-examine.

CROSS-EXAMINATION by Mr. Moody:

Q. Then as I understand you, doctor, this man was sane before and since, but just at the particular instant he shot Prescott?

A. You mean just for an instant?

Q. Yes.

A. No, I think that the time was longer than an instant. I think that Mr. Banks was so confused in thought by the very disturbing circumstances of the episode that his mind became confused, his mental stability was broken down for a time varying from a few moments to several minutes, but that he then recovered his mental normality again, though still in a more or less confused condition mentally.

Q. Well, what is it that would excite this man to this immediate spasm?

A. Why, the tragic circumstances in which he was placed with somebody trying to break into his house, with his own life and the life of his wife in danger; a man who was at that time, as the evidence indicates, worn down by anxiety and worry and sleeplessness for months prior to the occurrence of this episode.

Q. Yes, then whether they were or not trying to break into his house, if he thought so that would be sufficient to make him crazy, is that right?

A. That is sufficient to disturb his mind in that particular person and on that particular occasion. I don't say that the same circumstances would make everybody crazy or anybody crazy.

Q. Well, then I understand that this peculiar or particular kind of insanity that this man is suffering is just something that arises on the instant and then goes away, is that right?

A. Well, varying from a few moments to several minutes, as I said, yes, that is quite correct, quite correct. I don't think that Mr. Banks was insane prior to the 16th of March and I don't think he has been insane subsequent to the 16th of March.

Q. And you don't think that he is insane now?

A. I do not.

Q. Now what would you say about the mentality of a man three or four hours before a homicide that he was charged with committing, that he would write a letter to officers and tell them not to come to his house and if they did there would be bloodshed, and that when he saw the officers coming to the house he went out and got a rifle and told somebody else to open the door and within a few seconds shot at him, would you say a man like that was sane or insane?

A. Why he might be sane preceding the occurrence of the shooting and he might be insane at the time of the shooting.

Q. Well then, in other words, this preparation, getting ready for this event, isn't any evidence of an insane mind?

A. No, if it is true.

Mr. Moody: *That is all.*

REDIRECT-EXAMINATION by Mr. Lonergan

Q. Assuming the fact that a man had made preparations, Doctor, to take a trip up into the mountains and had packed his valise suitcase with clothes for that purpose and laid down his rifle which he intended to take along and his revolver in a holster and a cartridge belt which he intended to take along, and assuming someone came to the house and endeavored to break in, would a man then in that state of confusion and that state of insanity which you have explained be likely to grab a gun?"

A. Why, I think he would, yes.

Mr. Lonergan: *I think that is all, Doctor.*

The Court called a short recess. When court resumed the defense called Dr. B. F. Scaife, another psychologist, to testify. Mr. Lonergan began the direct-examination.

Q. Where do you reside, please?

A. Eugene.

Q. Are you a regularly licensed and practicing physician and surgeon in the State of Oregon?

A. Yes, yes.

Q. Had you practiced your profession before coming to Oregon?

A. At Saylor Springs, I had charge of a sanatorium, a resort for seventeen years. That's in southern Illinois, Clay County about a hundred miles south of St. Louis. And then later on for a short time in St. Louis and then came here.

Q. Have you specialized in any branch of the profession?

A. I couldn't say that I did. I perhaps have had more experience than the average in mental cases.

Q. Have you been called upon to give an opinion with reference to the condition of persons as to their sanity?

A. Yes, quite often.

Q. Did you have an opportunity, Doctor, to meet Llewellyn A. Banks, one of the defendants in this case?

A. Yes.

Q. And where was it that you first met him?

A. In the county jail. I think it was Thursday night.

Q. And did you have an opportunity to talk with him, to examine him and to observe him?

A. Yes, for I think it was something over three hours.

Q. Did you also have the opportunity of being present here in the courtroom and hearing his testimony on the witness stand?

A. Yes.

Q. I will ask you then, Doctor, from you observation and examination and from hearing his testimony here in the courtroom, and statements that have been made from the witness stand by him, whether or not you have formed an opinion as to whether or not on the 16th day of March, 1933, at the time of the shooting of George Prescott, that the defendant Llewellyn A. Banks was sane or insane?

A. I do not think at that time that he was sane.

Q. Will you say to the jury what in your opinion was the form of insanity suffered by the defendant Llewellyn A. Banks at the time of the happening of this episode?

A. I think it was what we call a transitory mania.

Q. And what is transitory mania?

A. Well, it is a type of mania that the authorities give as frenzied, excited, explosive type. That a patient in that condition seems to have an irresistible impulse to accomplish something, whether it is homicide, suicide or whatever flashes into his mind at that time.

Mr. Lonergan: *I believe you may cross-examine.*

CROSS-EXAMINATION by Mr. Moody:

Q. Did you know Mr. Banks before this trial?

A. No, sir.

Q. And you made your examination here in Eugene in the jail?

A. Yes.

Q. And you heard his testimony on the stand?

A. Yes.

Q. Then you based your opinion entirely and exclusively upon the testimony of Mr. Banks and your examination and observation of him?

A. Yes.

Q. Now what did you call this kind of insanity he had on March 16th?

A. Transitory mania is the term used in the books.

Q. But it is a fact, Doctor, that all the evidence on which you are relying in order to reach the conclusion you have stated is the examination that you made of Mr. Banks two or three days ago and your observation at that time and his testimony on the stand?

A. Yes.

Q. Well, how long does this transitory insanity last?

A. Varies. Sometimes only a few minutes, sometimes a few hours.

Q. Well, have you any evidence of the things that you have seen upon which to draw a conclusion that he was insane a minute or two before he shot Prescott?

A. Yes.

Q. What?

A. The violent strain that came over him and the very fact that all through his life there has been a weave, as it were, of some mental condition that wasn't exactly right, and the very fact that he had been under this severe strain so long and he saw his wife holding the door and a man trying to break in, why I think most any of us would ---

Q. You think that would make him insane whether—

A. Yes, it was sufficient.

Q. I will ask you what the modern authorities say upon the question of this transitory insanity?

A. Oh, I judge they differ but I think the greater number of them think there is and it is described.

Q. Well, it is a fact is it not that a great many—that many of the modern authorities say that this idea of transitory insanity is unsound?

A. Some say so, others don't. There is a disagreement on that. I am going by my own experience, the things that I have seen.

Q. Yes, and this temporary insanity is a doctrine or a rule that was adopted by the old doctors, that is that has been in existence for some time?

A. Yes, it has.

Q. But since that time other writers have thought that such a theory was fallacious?

A. Yes, there has always been new theories come out and I have seen many of them come out and used and dropped and discarded. The old theories as a rule have stood the test.

Q. But you put it exclusively upon the fact that he had a transitory insanity?

A. Yes.

Q. Now isn't it a fact that that theory of transitory insanity has been entirely exploded?

A. No.

Mr. Moody: *That is all.*

On Tuesday May 16th the defense rested its case. In the state's case in rebuttal Moody produced three doctors for the state.

DIRECT-EXAMINATION by Mr. Moody

Q. Doctor C.I. Drummond, what experience have you had with reference to the treatment and consideration and observation of cases of mental disease? Sit up, Doctor, straight up.

Mr. Lonergan: *What is that?*

The Court: *He told him to sit up straight.*

Mr. Moody: *I told him to sit up.*

Mr. Lonergan: *I see, I didn't understand.*

The Court: *Well, he has now straightened up.*

A. I have charge of the patients against whom insanity charges have been brought. And I have examined sixty or seventy-five patients last year.

Q. I will ask you whether or not the defendant Mr. Llewellyn A. Banks has been under your daily observation since he was incarcerated in the Jackson County jail?

A. Perhaps two or three times a week.

Q. I will ask you if you heard his testimony on the trial of this case?

A. Yes, sir.

Q. Well, I will ask you whether in your opinion from the observation that you have made of Mr. Banks and of hearing all his testimony, whether on March 16, 1933 he was sane or insane?

A. He was sane.

Q. I will ask you what is this transitory insanity that these other doctors have referred to.

A. I don't believe there is such a thing as transitory insanity, for such a short period as mentioned.

Q. Now I will ask you whether or not the modern writers and authors upon this question of transitory insanity have approved or disapproved of that original doctrine?

A. All—practically all I have read—have disapproved it.

Mr. Moody: *You may Cross-Examine.*

Mr. Lonergan's cross-examination failed to change the Doctor's mind. The Examination ended in a stalemate. Neither side proved much.

Mr. Moody's next witness in rebuttal was Dr. George I. Hurley. Mr. Moody established early in the doctor's testimony his credentials for practicing medicine and surgery. Clearly he had dealt with people having mental diseases.

Q. I will ask you from your observation of him in court, and you did see him, and from the testimony that you have heard adduced here and his story, as to whether or not on March 16, 1933 he was sane or insane?

A. I would say he was sane.

Q. In what manner do the modern authorities in medicine or on mental diseases treat the question of transitory insanity as compared with some of the older writers?

A. Well I think the modern writers are more inclined to strike it from the list of insanity.

Mr. Moody: You may cross-examine.

CROSS-EXAMINATION By Mr. Lonergan:

Q. There is such a thing as transitory mania?

A. Insanity to us means more, somewhat of a continuity of action and thought. We can hardly conceive of an insane person just momentarily. I prefer to use other terms rather that just that particular term.

Q. Well there are many authorities who have attempted to define insanity.

A. Yes, in a way, and they apologize usually for it.

Q. Well, doctors usually apologize for lots of things they write don't they?

A. Perhaps, so.

The Court: Don't include lawyers in that.

Mr. Lonergan: Even lawyers sometimes, Your Honor, yes.

Q. I am speaking about his experiences, his contacts, the things he lives through as "external pressure? Will you concede that things of that kind might bring on a condition of mania?

A. Why, I think troubles of the ---yes, a deterioration of the mind, might result in mania but I doubt if it could bring it on like that and off again (witness snapping fingers).

Q. At least there are many reputable authorities who agree that there is such a condition?

A. In the older books you will find it, yes.

Q. Isn't it true that there are a number of modern writers and authorities on nervous and mental diseases that have defined some of those cases that occurred in WWI at the front as transitory mania?

A. Well, I am not so sure about that. We call them mostly hysteria, fright.

184

Q. Which is a form of insanity, hysteria?

A. Well I think it isn't. Yes, sometimes it is, yes.

Q. Yes and recognized as a form of insanity?

A. Yes sir.

Mr. Lonergan: *That is all.*

Mr. Moody's next witness was Dr. W.C. Rebham, of Spring-field, a licensed physician and surgeon.

Q. You have heard all of Mr. Banks' testimonies haven't you?

A. Yes sir.

Q. Now from such observation and from the hearing of such testimony and from such facts, in your opinion on March 16, 1933 was Mr. Banks sane or insane?

A. It is my opinion that he was sane.

Q. Now you heard Dr. Josephi and Dr. Scaife testify, did you?

A. Yes.

Q. Well state now whether or not in your opinion that that question of transitory insanity now exists as in the older rule of it?

A. There are so many opinions on that. It is a little bit difficult to say. I think that it's recognized among the older writers but I think the newer writers are inclined to discard it.

As the court case was drawing to a close the prosecution produced a score of witnesses who testified that the reputation of Banks was "bad," while Officer Prescott was mild mannered and peaceful, with a good reputation. On Thursday the 18th both sides rested their cases. The jury was dismissed until 2pm when the closing arguments would commence.

When the jury adjourned, the judge had a few words for the lawyers. "I want to be sure that the right interpretation is placed on the law by both sides of the case in appealing to the jury. The statute holds that an officer with a warrant for a man's arrest may break open any door or portal if entrance is refused. The defense is introducing two pleas in the case, 'temporary insanity' and 'self-defense.' The defendant would be able to plead self-defense only in the event that the officer was using more force than necessary or had threatened the defendant and was attempting to commit a felony on his person. It will be for the jury to decide whether or not this was the case."

When the jury returned, the state and the defense launched into nearly two days of final arguments. A reporter for the *Mail Tribune* characterized the presentation by Mr. Moody, as conversational until the end, when his voice was raised.

Mr. Moody: *"Where is the excuse that defense counsel can point to, in justification of this outrageous and unconscionable murder? Nobody was pestering Banks but his creditors. [He was] sued 31 times. [This] is no justification for Banks to murder Prescott."*

"The only question before this jury is whether or not Llewellyn A. Banks, and his wife aiding, killed George Prescott with deliberation, premeditation and preparation."

"Banks was cold-blooded enough to plan the murder but too cowardly to go to the door to open it. Banks was a good marksman. He stood 35 or 40 feet away and hit a man in the heart, through a crack in the door, four or five inches wide. Banks shot George Prescott with a nasty, vicious mushroom bullet that civilized nations have barred from use in modern warfare. But his crazy theory was also hit. Dr. Josephi said he was crazy when he pulled the trigger. He must have had a lucid moment in his "transitory mania" when he shot so straight and true. He was not crazy then nor is he now."

Mr. Moody claimed that Banks showed no sympathy for Prescott, and that Banks was selfish and egotistical. He then declared that Mrs. Banks was guilty too. "She acted jointly, deliberatively, and premeditatedly in the slaying." Mr. Moody summed up his case on Thursday afternoon, March 18th. The next day the jury would hear the defense.

Another crowded courtroom awaited Banks' lawyers sitting between Mr. and Mrs. Banks at the prisoners' bar was their 12-year-old daughter, Ruth May, quiet, and curly-haired. Close by sat Bank's foremost advocate and brother-in-law Charles P. Moran, responsible for funding the lawyers representing Banks. When defense lawyers began by attacking Jackson County's district attorney Codding, Banks smiled, but otherwise remained expressionless. His wife sat with a bowed head. The jury alertly leaned towards the speakers.

Mr. Lonergan and attorney Charles Hardy of Eugene led the defense, plunging into their summations. Mr. Lonergan claimed that Banks was temporarily insane when he pulled the trigger. He had tried to get corrupt county officials to resign using his newspaper as a bullhorn, but when they didn't resign they persecuted Banks and it affected his mind adversely. Mr. Hardy attempted to prove that Banks was a victim of "organized persecution," and that the crowd persecuting Banks were the ones who should have been charged with syndicalism.

Mr. Lonergan added, "Banks was a hounded man, staying in his home for ten days before the tragedy to avoid trouble, planning to leave for the mountains to save his own life. Finally, when he saw Prescott trying to break into his home to get him, Banks lost his reason." Lonergan pleaded with the jury to free the old couple so that they could raise their daughter Ruth May.

The defense then produced its own witnesses to show Banks was a good man. Standing up for his good character

Ruth Mae Banks
Photo from the Southern Oregon Historical Society collection

were: Earl H. Fehl, W.H. Gore, Dr. J.F. Reddy, V.J. Emerick, Dr. F.G. Swedenburg and Mrs. Ariel Burton Pomeroy. The latter stated she had "never heard anyone doubt Mr. Banks' reputation for truth."

"When I sit down," Mr. Lonergan said, "the lips of the defendants will be sealed. The state has one more chance at you before you take the fate of the old couple to the jury room. But we'll be waiting—waiting—waiting for your decision." His presentation was so moving it brought the ladies in the front of the crowded courtroom to tears.

Mr. Moody in his rebuttal on Saturday morning reviewed the case point by point. He waived the bloody warrant in front of the jury. He said that the defense witnesses who had claimed to see a gun in Prescott's hand had obviously lied. Mr. Moody ended by saying Llewellyn A. Banks deliberately shot George Prescott, and Edith Banks was his accomplice.

When Mr. Moody had finished, Judge Skipworth addressed the jury. His instructions took over an hour. He explained that Mr. Banks and Mrs. Banks were jointly indicted and tried, yet the jury was to "consider the case of each defendant separately." They held the authority to imprison one and set the other free. The judge also explained the law surrounding a plea of self-defense and insanity.

The judge then described the verdicts the jury could choose. The different verdicts had been printed on forms and handed to the jury.

1) First degree murder requiring the death penalty.

2) First degree murder with a recommendation for life in prison.

3) Second degree murder

4) Third degree murder-guilty of Manslaughter.

5) Not guilty by reason of Insanity.

6) Not guilty.

"Now, Ladies and Gentlemen of the jury, this is Saturday afternoon, this completes the instruction of the Court as to the law. It is your duty to decide this case fairly and squarely upon the evidence that has been introduced in this case and upon the law as given you by the Court."

Jury's Decision

At 3:30 pm on Saturday, the jurors retired to the third floor of the Lane County Courthouse for deliberation. By nine o'clock that night they still hadn't reached a verdict so the seven men and five women spent the night in the courthouse. Breakfast was at 7:30 a.m. in the dining room of the Osburn Hotel. After breakfast the jury returned to the third floor of the courthouse.

By 1:30 p.m, after 22 hours of deliberation, the jury called in the bailiffs. They had made their decision. Judge Skipworth summoned the state and defense counsels and the defendants to the courthouse for the reading of the verdict. Also hurrying to the courtroom were Medford citizens, members of the Good Government Congress, Eugene residents, young lawyers, and newspaper reporters.

Jury foreman J.A. Phelps presented the verdicts to Judge Skipworth. A hush fell over the room when the judge was about to read the verdicts. Judge Skipworth asked the defendants to please stand. Then he read the verdicts aloud. The jury had decided that L.A. Banks was guilty of second-degree murder with recommendation of life imprisonment. Mrs. Edith Robertine Banks was found not guilty. On hearing the judgment Mr. Banks stared ahead glassy eyed, while Mrs. Banks bowed her head and quietly sobbed. Mr. Banks eventually smiled at her and gently patted her arm. Mrs. Banks' sister-in-law wept while her husband George Moran helped her from the courtroom.

The jury filed from the room. Jury foreman Phelps refused to discuss the jury's balloting with reporters. He and his colleagues had agreed not to discuss the reasons for their decision.

Robert Ruhl's *Mail Tribune* proclaimed a "Great Victory. This paper wants Mr. Moody to know that the law-abiding people of Medford and Jackson County appreciate this, and are deeply grateful to him for what he has done —the invaluable public service to this community which he has performed. It is a service they will never forget. In our opinion the verdict was eminently a just one, and reflects great credit upon the good sense and clear thinking of the members of the jury which delivered it."

Judge Skipworth set the formal sentencing of L. A. Banks for August 14, 1933. Between May and August Robert Ruhl knew that there was still another injustice that needed some answers. Who was responsible for the ballot thefts, and what would their punishments be?

Ballot Theft Trials

Oregon's attorney general appointed Assistant Attorney General Ralph E. Moody to prosecute the Jackson county ballot theft cases. Once again, Skipworth was to be the judge. Moody's first ballot theft case was against Arthur La Dieu, the former business manager for Banks' newspaper. Mr. Moody hoped to set up a framework of evidence that the prosecution could use against the other five conspirators—Walter Jones, mayor of Rogue River; John Glenn, jailer at Medford; Thomas Brecheen, political leader from Ashland; Gordon Schermerhorn, former Medford sheriff; and Earl Fehl, publisher and judge from Medford.

Even though the circumstances behind each trial were different the overall case against the six was similar. The trial against La Dieu set the stage. Mr. Moody charged that he was, a part of a conspiracy to steal ballots in order to prevent a recount of the election results from 1932. Bags of ballots had been dropped in the Rogue River or burned in the courthouse furnace—10,000 ballots in all.

Since there had been a slew of confessions, La Dieu didn't have much chance of acquittal.

The defense was reduced to trying to discredit the witnesses. But the witnesses stuck to their stories. The evidence against La Dieu was overwhelming. When it came to the summation Mr. Moody said, "This country believes in the principal that the majority shall rule, and we have maintained one of the best governments in the world. [La Dieu and his conspirators] struck at the very foundation of our government." It took the jury seven hours to decide La Dieu's verdict—guilty.

Similar verdicts were handed down to the mayor of Rogue River and Thomas Brecheen. Even though John Glenn was charged on the basis of mostly the same evidence, he was somehow declared, "not guilty" by the jury. Mr. Moody found this verdict hard to believe. "The State regrets the miscarriage of justice with the acquittal of Glenn, who was unquestionably guilty." He thought the jury was too sympathetic, swayed by the fact that Glenn might lose his pension. Gordon Schermerhorn was next on the docket and was found guilty.

After the first convictions, The *Medford Mail Tribune* wrote, "The leaders of the Good Government Congress organized to carry out one of the most diabolical plots ever attempted in order to hold control of public offices. They planned and executed the breaking into the courthouse and stealing the ballots of the last election in order to prevent a recount. Testimony of the participants has shown that L.A. Banks, County Judge Fehl and others were leading the revolution. Had they succeeded the end might easily have been virtual anarchy in Jackson County."

Judge Fehl's case was next. He won a change of venue to Klamath County, where the trial was held in the courthouse. The prosecution presented evidence that the judge had tampered with the ballots, and that he, Banks, and others led the conspiracy to steal the ballots. The defense attorneys didn't manage much of a rebuttal. It took all of 20 minutes for the jury to decide that Judge Earl Fehl was guilty in the ballot theft case.

Fehl, La Dieu, and Jones were sentenced to four years in the State Penitentiary. Schermerhorn was given three years, and Brecheen eighteen months. Assistant Attorney General Ralph Moody moved that the judge dismiss all other charges. "With the conviction of L.A. Banks for murder and conviction of the leaders in the ballot theft the state feels that the situation had been entirely cleared up. The state has prosecuted the chief cases and does not want to carry that prosecution to the degree that it will become persecution."

Banks' Punishment

L lewellyn Banks had been allowed to stay in the Lane County jail until final sentencing. During that time he had undergone an operation and was being monitored for stress. By August 14th he had recovered. That is when Judge George F. Skipworth had scheduled to formally sentence Llewellen A. Banks.

Llewellyn A. Banks, along with his defense attorneys Charles A. Hardy and Frank Lonergan met in the Lane County courthouse with the Honorable G.F. Skipworth presiding as Circuit Judge, and the state being represented by Assistant Attorney General R.E. Moody.

The Court: Anything further in this case before I impose sentence?

Mr. Lonergan: We desire to object to the passing of sentence at this time on the ground that the Court has no jurisdiction to pass sentence and that the passing of sentence at this time would be a legal nullity.

The Court: The objection is overruled.

The Court: Stand up, Mr. Banks. Have you anything to say why sentence should no be imposed at this time?

The Defendent: My lawyer will speak for me.

The Court: Of course there is only one sentence that may be imposed on a conviction of murder in the second degree. It is the judgment of the Court that you be imprisoned in the penitentiary of the State of Oregon for the full term and during your natural life. You are remanded to the custody of the sheriff to be conveyed to the penitentiary."

He was received at the Salem prison on August 14, 1933. He had in his possession $1.05, a good luck piece, a penknife, and a suitcase of clothes. His case file number at the penitentiary was 12697.

Curiously, on the next day August 15, 1933, Earl Fehl was received at the penitentiary. His case file number was 12698, the next number after Banks.

The *Oregonian* felt that the Jackson County rebellion was the result of the Depression. The county's problems would not have been so bad had it not been for the agonizing economic conditions. If the community had spent as much time solving economic problems as fighting the agitators, the whole political maelstrom might have been averted.

The *Oregonian* missed the point: Sure, the economic conditions helped catapult Banks and Fehl into a position of power. But the agitators needed to be confronted. Their downfall was due to the determination and diligent journalism of Robert W. Ruhl. Ruhl who faced tough economic times too, but he didn't sell his paper. He stuck it out, and fought back against the dictator with editorial after editorial. Ruhl's *Mail Tribune* didn't let the majority of people be misled by a dangerously, ill-informed minority.

A Pulitzer Prize

On May 8, 1934 Columbia University announced the Pulitzer Prize winners for 1933. The *Medford Mail Tribune* and its editor Robert W. Ruhl won the gold medal worth $500, "the most distinguished and meritorious public service rendered by an American newspaper during the year."

The Pulitzer panel praised the *Medford Mail Tribune* for fighting off the attempts of L.A. Banks, the editor of a rival newspaper, to establish an armed dictatorship in Jackson County.

The *Medford Mail Tribune* can truly be heralded as the hero in its courageous stand against tyranny and oppression. The coveted Pulitzer Prize, medal, now is proudly displayed in the offices of the *Medford Mail Tribune*.

The Pulitzer Journalism Award Certificate presented to the *Medford Mail Tribune*; signed, June 5, 1934

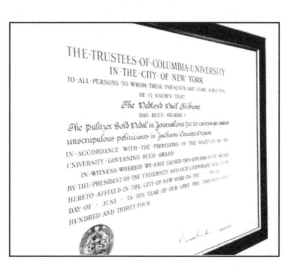

The Joseph Pulitzer Gold Medal in Journalism
awarded by Columbia University to the *Medford Mail Tribune*.

Blast from Prison

Not everyone felt that Ruhl deserved a prize. Llewellyn A. Banks wrote from prison, "Now behind prison walls, I make this solemn statement—When I am returned to liberty, I will owe it to my God, to my state, and to my nation, to abolish forever, the institution of iniquity—a sordid, soulless, diabolical controlled press."

Not long after the issuance of the Pulitzer Prize, rumors began to spread that Banks might be released in December 1934 after serving only 15 months in prison.

Banks' sister's husband, George F. Moran, had singlehandedly convinced prominent Oregon citizens to sign a petition for Banks to be released from prison. The petition was presented to outgoing Governor Meier in the hope that he would pardon Banks. The thought of Banks being released aroused bitter feelings in Medford. Ruhl and other business leaders composed letters urging the governor not to do this. Ruhl also consulted with Ralph Moody, the state prosecutor who had sent Banks to prison. The powerful people that Moran had corralled were so influential that for a while it appeared that Banks might be freed. Moody talked to the governor and assured Ruhl there would be no pardon. Ruhl relieved, wrote a letter back to Moody:

Dear Dick:

Your letter about Banks just received. A week ago I would have been wild. Now only amused, for I have read many of them similarly inspired by your friend Moran. Don't tell me he is a go-getter. I know it. He could sell J. P. Morgan the Brooklyn Bridge. Imagine his getting similar letters from the Catholic archbishop of Oregon, one of the state's leading editors. Irvine of the Portland Journal, two leaders of the bar in Portland, an ex U.S. Senator, an ex-ambassador to Poland, the former president of the state senate and scores of others. To me, knowing Banks and his case as I do, the achievement is simply paralyzing, incredible, gigantic, Ko-loss-al! Only the hardest kind of work, intensive, persistent, prevented Governor Meier from pardoning this convicted murderer, after having served 15 months of his properly imposed life term! And some wonder why the crime wave in this country is the scandal of the civilized world.

Moran worked quietly and effectively. The first news of the situation came to me over long distance from Portland about ten days ago, I got up in my shirt tail from bed, where I had been cavorting with the flu for six days and stayed up, most of the time at the phone, for three days and nights, until the thing was scotched, and such an outrage against justice and ordinary decency prevented. My Dear Richard, Banks murdered a man in cold blood, a friend of mine, one of the best peace officers Southern Oregon ever had. He was given a fair trial, not here but in Eugene, 200 miles away, where public sentiment was favorable to him. He was defended by two of the best criminal lawyers in the state—strictly speaking he should have been hung—the jury compromised on life—the trial was reviewed by the state supreme court and upheld in every particular. What possible excuse then for his pardon and release? Absolutely none-except political influence and money behind him. I feel sorry for his wife and family. I don't blame Moran particularly for doing what he can for the brother of his wife. I am in a sense sorry for Banks, or any man like him—able, forceful, shrewd but as dangerous as a saw teeth tiger. I know him. Were he set free, it is as certain as the night following day there would be another tragedy. He may be crazy-I don't know -but the insanity plea interjected at the trial was not accepted. Crazy or sane, the only place for him is where he can do no further harm. If he were released by an out-going governor, we might as well close the courts, discharge all peace officers in this state and turn over things entirely to the Good Governments, their calf skin vests and sawed off shotguns.

I want to forget this Banks case and most of the people here-abouts do too. But damned if the Banks bunch will allow it. I am even getting anonymous communications today defending him and maintaining he was a sacrifice to the power trust, broken on the wheel of greed and avarice. Great Lord, I sometimes think that not only was Banks crazy but everyone who came in contact with him lost their minds. No one goaded Banks into anything. He was the goader, the leader, the John Brown. He was the sole cause of all the trouble. The real mystery to me is that anyone really knowing Banks-and his own sister should-could wish him to be anywhere but where he is.

"Sincerely Yours, Robert Ruhl

Banks was destined to remain in prison for the rest of his life.

Epilogue

Llewellyn A. Banks

While awaiting his final sentencing Llewellyn began writing his book *Weighed in the Balance*. In 1933 while in the penitentiary he published the book. In that book he claimed that democracy in the USA had become a dictatorship. He also expressed strong racist feelings against the Jews— much like Hitler in Germany.

After losing his chance at clemency in 1934, Banks would serve out his entire life sentence at the state penitentiary. He worked in the prison laundry, library, and machine shop. His jail records include many confrontations, and arrogant behavior. His letters to the outside world displayed such vehemence towards elected officials that his writings were curtailed and censored. Even letters that were written to him were sometimes withheld as a form of punishment.

Banks asserted that there had been attempts to murder him. He and Judge Fehl collaborated on one so-called murder attempt. Banks claimed the sugar he kept in his cell had been spiked with poison. He blamed this on Ralph E. Moody—who hadn't been in the prison at all. In the sugar poison case Warden J. W. Lewis wrote in a letter to governor Charles H. Martin, "We have carefully examined every phase of the matter and are not at all convinced that an attempt was made to poison Mr. Banks at any time."

While performing his duties he took every opportunity to seek parole. All of them failed, because he refused to accept responsibility for his crime. He never thought he had made a mistake by shooting Officer Prescott. His inability to understand his culpability was frustrating to his family and those who supported his parole attempts. He continued to make hateful remarks about Ralph E. Moody, the Oregon legal system, and the Jewish community. These comments led a prison doctor to say Banks was psychotic. The doctor felt Banks "would harm someone if he should be let out into society."

His wife Edith tried to stay close to Llewellyn by remaining in Salem for a few years. But Llewellyn blamed Edith for his loss of money from a government claim he had filed in the early 1920s. He felt Edith had sold him out for a settlement behind his back after the 1933 trial in Eugene. Relations between the two soured. Even his daughter Ruth Mae remained estranged. Both she and Edith stopped writing Llewellyn in the penitentiary.

Towards the end, Banks suffered many months of excruciating pain from cancer. In March 1945 Banks had an operation in Eugene to address the pain. After the operation his pain seemed to subside for a while and he made a concerted effort to recover. But he never left the hospital. Llewellyn died on September 21, 1945, at the age of 75.

Edith Banks and Ruth Mae

Edith and Ruth Mae' lived in Salem for a couple of years after the trial then moved briefly to Corvallis. From Corvallis Edith was hired by Chester Banks who ran an orchard packinghouse in Monrovia, California. It seemed neither Edith nor Ruth Mae were able to forgive Llewellyn for his accusations against Edith. The pair lived in Monrovia, until Edith's death.

Joe Cave

The first grand juries in the incident of Everett Dahack's death had exonerated all of the officers involved during the moonshine raid in 1930. Then in late 1933, as a result of a continuous barrage of newspaper attacks by Fehl and Banks, a new grand jury was formed to investigate the affair. That jury accused Joe Cave of manslaughter. This grand jury was suspect, because both Judge Fehl and Llewellyn Banks had visited the courtroom during their deliberations. Because of their presence another grand jury was called in January 1934 to determine if Joe Cave was guilty.

The new grand jury went to the scene of the killing twice. They heard twenty-one witnesses, and studied "all maps and records." They concluded, "From the consideration of the entire case we find there is a possibility that a shot from the rifle used by Joe Cave caused the tragedy. But it was an unavoidable accident. The officer was attempting within his rights, to apprehend a person fleeing from the commission of a felony, and from where the shot was fired could not see the deceased (Dahack)." The judge said, "Your findings should be regarded as final."

The Joe Cave incident had been a hammer that both Banks and Fehl had used relentlessly for three years. But, the new jury did what the original one had done—found Joe Cave innocent.

Judge Earl Fehl

While in prison between August 1933 and May 1936, two incidents hurt Fehl's chance for an earlier parole. His first scheme was to dictate a pamphlet to his wife Electa, presenting his side of the ballot box thefts. Electa distributed the pamphlets on street corners in Medford. She was arrested, but later released when it was found out that her husband Earl was behind the scheme. The pamphlet was called "Black Political Plot Exposed, Who Stole the Ballots?" Fehl's second problem arose when visiting his cellblock neighbor,

Llewellyn Banks. Fehl said that the sugar Banks used to sweeten his cocoa seemed to be poisoned. An exhaustive study concluded the claim was false.

Earl Fehl was finally paroled on May 6, 1936. On December 20, 1937 he was judged to be insane and committed to the State Hospital. He was discharged on July 1, 1942. When out of the Hospital Fehl rented out his Herald Building. Electa Fehl died in April 1949. Earl remarried and lived at 504 so. Oakdale Ave, Medford until his death. Fehl was 77 years old when he passed away on January 29, 1962.

Oregon Attorney Frank John Lonergan

After the Jackson County trials his wife died in January 1935. They were childless. A Republican, he served in the Oregon legislature from Multnomah County 1939 to 1941. He helped author a pension bill and was a candidate for governor in 1934. In 1945 he became Multnomah County Circuit Judge and was a prominent member of the Elks Lodge. He died at St. Vincent's Hospital in Portland on October 4, 1961. He was 79.

Oregon Assistant Attorney General Ralph Elmo Moody

During or after the trials in 1933 Ralph Moody married Regina Elizabeth Johnson of Ashland. After the Banks case he authored a public utility district law and was involved in legal battles relating to federal pricing laws. Mr. Moody was noted for working on complicated cases, and had a tremendous knowledge of constitutional law. He and his wife Regina were childless. On September 29, 1955 Mr. Moody passed away at the age of 88.

Edith L. Prescott

Constable Prescott's wife, Edith L. Prescott, died November 12, 1952 at the age of 80. She had lived in Medford for 34 years and Gold Hill about two and a half years. She was a member of the Rebekah Lodge. She is buried alongside of her husband, George, in the Medford I.O.O.F. Eastwood Cemetery, S.W. Circle Lot 20.

The Llewellyn Banks' Home

This house is also known as the Root-Banks home. Orchardist John M. Root built the home about 1914.

At the corner of Peach Street and West Main Street in Medford, Banks purchased the place between 1926 and 1927. The home has since served as a university club, a rental, and a doctor's home. In the 1960s it was converted to commercial use. Then it was used as a lumber company office, a home for homeless teens, and a computer software store. In 1994 the home was placed on the National Register of Historic Places. Recently the building has been in disrepair. Some occupants refuse to stay there at night, fearing the eerie and strange sounds—possibly ghosts?

Lane County Courthouse—Razed in 1959.

Robert Waldo Ruhl

Ruhl and his newspaper were awarded the nation's highest professional honor in journalism—the Pulitzer Prize. The certificate reads, "Be It Known That The *Medford Mail Tribune* Has Been Awarded The Pulitzer Gold Medal in Journalism for its

Robert W. Ruhl,
Former publisher, The *Medford Mail Tribune*

campaign against unscrupulous politicians in Jackson County, Oregon."

Governor Martin thought so highly of Ruhl he appointed him to a nine-year term on the State Board of Higher Education in 1936. Ruhl served as president of the Oregon Editorial Conference in 1936. He was also a member of the Sigma Delta Chi, an honorary fraternity for professional journalists.

Robert Ruhl's editorials expressed a liberal attitude and were always honest in their presentation. Ruhl approached dissension with "calm determination," according to an editorial in the *Medford Mail Tribune*, "His duty as an editor was the great motivating factor throughout Robert W. Ruhl's long and distinguished career, and beside it all else was secondary." Ruhl supported candidates he thought capable of holding office. Mr. Ruhl preferred to be called an "Independent." Editor George Turnbull wrote in 1939, "This independent policy has been followed through the years, as a political attitude. It is far from being as strange doctrine now as it was about 20 years ago." Ruhl retired as editor of the *Mail Tribune* in the 1950s, when Eric Allen Jr. took over the position. Ruhl and his wife lived in San Francisco until his death in 1967. Ruhl was survived by his wife Mabel and two married daughters, Roxane and Alicia Ann.

In 1973 Mabel Ruhl gave an endowment to the Journalism Department at the University of Oregon. Ruhl's endowment is used to fund the annual Ruhl Symposium. Each year eminent journalists are invited to give lectures. The symposium has been a popular University event since 1978. Speakers in 2015 were Karen Pensiero, Editor for Newsroom Standards at the *Wall Street Journal*, and Eric Liu, former speechwriter for President Bill Clinton. Mrs. Ruhl's hope was that the lectures would contribute to "the development of students into dedicated journalists. I feel it is especially important today that we restore in this field of journalism a greater sense of ethics, responsibility and dedication."

Acknowledgments

I am indebted to my editor, William L. Sullivan, for his encouragement and patience in turning my rambling manuscript into an interesting story, and with the precision of a surgeon correcting my grammatical errors. He did a lot of work to make my manuscript readable.

The layout, covers and final editing was done by Pat Edwards of *Groundwaters* Publishing—a gifted publisher.

Further, I had help from all these sources and people:

- Doctorial Dissertation by Jeffrey Max LaLande, *The Jackson County Rebellion 1932-1933* and other articles by LaLande.
- The University of Oregon:
    Microfilm Department
    Law Library, Jaye Anne Barlous, reference librarian
    Archives Department
    School of Journalism, Amy Pinkston
    Map Department
- Oregon State Archives in Salem; Austin Schulz, MA. CA.
- The Oregon Historical Society; their quarterly magazine and photographs, assisted by Scott Daniels.
- The Oregon Department of Corrections, in Salem, Oregon.
- Lane County Historical Society, assisted by Cheryl Roffe.
- Lane County Courthouse archives.
- Southern Oregon Historical Society, assisted by Rick Black.
- The Jackson County Genealogical Library, in Medford.
- The Oregon State Library in Salem, assisted by Dave Hegeman. Dave was a great help in getting a photograph of one of my favorite Oregon governors, Ben Olcott.

I read many books, and articles concerning the Rebellion. I had a few interviews, plus read many online sources. Of course, Oregon newspapers from 1900 to 1940 provided the bulk of information. Plus, I had access to the entire trial transcript, and I had obtained copies of the prison files on Llewellyn Banks and Earl Fehl.

About the Author

Joe Blakely lives with his wife, Saundra Miles in Eugene, Oregon. He has one son, Justin, and a stepson, Jonathan Baker. Mr. Blakely earned a degree in history from San Diego State College—while in college he excelled in the writing of history term papers.

Mr. Blakely retired from the office of public safety at the University of Oregon in 1999. After retirement he decided to write about Oregon history.

With the addition of his new book, *Rebellion, Murder and a Pulitzer Prize*, Mr. Blakely has written ten books about Oregon—seven histories and three historical fiction novels. Mr. Blakely says his best work is his biography of Oswald West, Oregon's rascally governor who wrote legislation in 1913 to set aside Oregon's beaches as a highway, thereby providing public access. His two Highway 101 coast books, *Lifting Oregon Out of the Mud: Building the Oregon Coast Highway* (2006) and *Building Oregon's Coast Highway 1936-1966: Straightening Curves and Uncorking Bottlenecks* (2014) on building the coast highway, have been most popular.

Mr. Blakely is currently working on a novel set in 1960, on Oregon's Coast Highway.

To contact Joe Blakely, you can write him at

PO Box 51561, Eugene, Oregon 97405.

Made in the USA
Monee, IL
07 July 2022